The Capable Company

The Capable Company

Building the capabilities that make strategy work

Richard L. Lynch, John G. Diezemann, and James F. Dowling

Blackwell
Publishing

350 Main Street, Malden, MA 02148-5020, USA
108 Cowley Road, Oxford OX4 1JF, UK
550 Swanston Street, Carlton, Victoria 3053, Australia

First published 2003 by Blackwell Publishing Ltd

Library of Congress Cataloging-in-Publication Data
Lynch, Richard L.
The capable company : building the capabilities that make strategy
work / Richard L. Lynch, John G. Diezemann, and James F. Dowling.
p. cm.
Includes bibliographical references and index.
ISBN 1-4051-1182-8 (pbk. : alk. paper)
1. Organizational effectiveness. 2. Strategic planning.
3. Organizational change. 4. Leadership. I. Diezemann, John.
II. Dowling, James F. III. Title.
HD58.9.L96 2003
658. 4–dc21   2002155059

A catalogue record for this title is available from the British Library.

Set in 10/12.5pt Baskerville
by Kolam Information Services Pvt. Ltd, Pondicherry, India
Printed and bound in the United Kingdom
by MPG Books, Bodmin, Cornwall

For further information on
Blackwell Publishing, visit our website:
http://www.blackwellpublishing.com

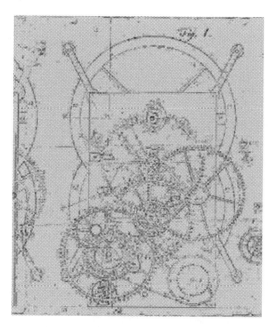

A sketch of the mechanism of H3 by Thomas Bradley (© RGO Archive).

In the seventeenth century thousands of sailors were shipwrecked at sea because they could not find their position. England recognized that the capability to determine the precise position of their ships at sea would give them maritime supremacy: crew safety, the avoidance of costly shipwrecks, faster time for trade routes, and advantages in military positioning. Scientists in England, France, and Italy knew that precise knowledge of the time at a home port would enable the capability. They also "knew" that no clock could ever remain accurate in harsh conditions at sea.

By 1727, England's John Harrison, a carpenter-turned-clockmaker, had made a portable clock with a "gridiron" pendulum, which consisted of nine alternating steel and brass rods to eliminate any effects of temperature changes. In the years that followed, he used this mechanism to make four timepieces. After three clock designs missed the mark, Harrison shed the clock idea and developed a completely different design – an accurate watch, a chronograph! This capability gave England supremacy over the seas for decades.

Contents

Figures

Tables

Preface

While meeting to discuss the outline for this book, we struggled with an initial concept or metaphor for the "Capable Company." As we played around with various constructs, including the gear metaphor ultimately chosen for the book, a flock of birds flew over the skylight. It dawned on us that a Capable Company is like the "V formation" of birds flying overhead. All the parts of this organization are synchronized with a common purpose and mission. Flying in this formation reduces wind resistance and helps the entire flock get farther with less energy. Every bird can lead and everyone aligns behind the leader. The flock knows when to move and has the ability to make rapid course corrections. This serendipitous observation led to a quick search on the Web using the key term "self-organizing mechanisms."

Indeed, the passing flock of migrating birds is not a freak in nature. As Margaret Wheatley observed in *Goodbye Command and Control*:

(the) impulse to organize so as to accomplish more is not only true of humans, but is found in all living systems. Every living thing seeks to create a world in which it can thrive. It does this by creating systems of relationships where all members of the system benefit from their connections. This movement toward organization, called self-organization in the sciences, is everywhere, from microbes to galaxies. Patterns of relationships form into effective systems of organization. Organization is a naturally occurring phenomenon. The world seeks organization, seeks its own effectiveness. And so do the people in our organizations. As a living system self-organizes, it develops shared understanding of what's important, what's acceptable behavior, what actions are required, and how these actions will get done. It develops channels of communication, networks of workers, and complex physical structures. And as the system develops, new capacities emerge from living and working together.

Yet this commonplace event in nature is difficult to replicate in the business world. Most companies struggle with orchestrated, systemic change.

In our work at leadership conferences and seminars and with client companies, we keep hearing common themes about failure to adapt to opportunities:

- Lack of leadership and direction in uncertain times.
- Failure to execute on the strategy.
- Leadership misalignment.
- Failure to exploit the value exchange across supplier and customer boundaries.
- Inability to regenerate the business.
- Lack of understanding of business "archetypes" and the constraints they impose.
- Support systems, especially rewards and compensation are not aligned to the strategy.
- Poor processes to adapt to change.

These symptoms reveal an underlying problem: when strategies are not translated into clear capabilities, strategy execution is left to one of three methods:

1 *Orderly Inaction* – waiting to be told what to do.
2 *Chaotic Action* – doing what you like to do.
3 *Strategic Improvisation* – guessing what to do.

Even if action is taken, individual programs such as balanced scorecards or e-commerce initiatives cannot be thought of as stand-alone programs. They are the components of a system (flock) that share a common destination. These projects (and their champions) must be aligned to reduce organization resistance, ready to lead or follow, and have the ability to make mid-course corrections in flight.

Our in-depth experiences in companies such as Analog Devices, Blyth, Emmis Communications, Ford Motor Company, GE Capital, Quantum

Technologies, StorageTek, TeleTech Holdings, and Viacom suggest a composite picture of how companies respond to an uncertain future. The key to success lies in the mundane but critical development of capabilities that make strategy work. When companies have the discipline to do this, they create their own self-organization mechanisms; quickly moving on new opportunities while competitors stare and wonder: "How did they know that and react so fast?"

There are many excellent books and theories on leadership, customer value, business architecture, balanced scorecards, and project management. Our contribution to the literature is to lay out a systematic and sustainable process for targeting and building those specific capabilities that take a company's strategy to action.

August 2002
Rich Lynch
John Diezemann
Jim Dowling

Acknowledgments

While many people contributed directly and indirectly to this book, several key individuals helped shape our thinking and provided constructive feedback on early versions of the manuscript.

First, we would like to thank Norm Smallwood and Dave Ulrich of Results-Based Leadership, Inc. for their groundbreaking work on leadership development; especially their work on the "leadership brand" and building "organization capabilities." *The Capable Company* was drafted in parallel with their book *Why the Bottom Line Isn't* (Wiley, 2003), and we benefited greatly from early reviews of their draft manuscripts. Norm also provided valuable guidance on chapter 4, "Make Strategy Visible," which is based in part on ideas he put forth in *Real-Time Strategy* (Wiley, 1993).

In the area of business architecture we are grateful to Dick Dooley; Joe Siebert, Chief Information Officer at Viacom; and the works of John Zachman for their insights into enterprise architecture and the role of information technology (IT).

We would also like to thank our colleagues Victor Agruso, David Altman, and Jim Intagliato for their input to our organization diagnostics. For tracking down the history of the Sans Souci house mentioned in chapter 8, thanks go to Carol Bacon, Director of the Tyngsboro Library in Massachusetts.

Since Capable Companies are known for taking vision to action, of equal importance to our theoretical underpinnings are the pragmatic contributions from the change champions in many of our client companies.

First, we would like to thank Dixon Thayer, Stu Silberman of the Ford Motor Company, Steve Snyder of Exult, and Mike Panowyk for their contributions to building an "advantaged business model." This formed our approach to our discussion on forging customer relationships in chapter 6.

At Quantum Technologies, we'd like to thank Syed Hussein and Glenn Moffett for their suggestions on capability gap analysis. We also thank Malana Slover at Blyth, Inc. for suggestions on executing a "CBA cycle."

At GE Capital, where we were part of the "Six Sigma design and launch team," we would like to thank Mike Markovits for his insights on what makes GE so unique and how the company builds organization capabilities so quickly.

Susan Curtis, Annette Woodham, and Roger Gaston of StorageTek and Laura Abiodun of the Brady Corporation deserve special mention for their help in creating a process to provide strategic focus and leadership alignment to strategy. Of special note, we thank Laura, along with Tom Lloyd, Mark Pinto (Cap Gemini Ernst & Young), and Deborah Voosen for their input to the "Capable Company Eye Chart" in chapter 4 and ideas for "action learning."

At the Gillette Company we thank Charlie DellaCroce, Jack Mastrianni, and Paul Butler for their input on strategy alignment and insights into Gillette history.

Finally, we extend our gratitude to our families and friends who put up with us once again as we focused our energies and attention on this project.

1 Introduction

If past history was all there was to the game, the richest people in the world would be librarians.

— Warren Buffet

Business leaders know a dirty little secret. Most companies don't flounder because of poor strategy. The culprit is poor execution of the game plan. If executives know this, why don't they do something about it? The problem is that strategic intent, written in the language of a few visionaries, gets lost when the rank and file tries to interpret it in operational ways.

The Capable Company provides the "Rosetta Stone" executives have been seeking: a systematic way to translate strategy into capabilities and projects. While some companies do this intuitively, this book lays out a repeatable process so that leaders at all levels can rapidly focus and align their actions — even as business conditions change — to build competitive advantage.

The New Business Reality

The whirlwind of change emanating from a globally connected world is testing the reach of many businesses. As a result, companies are scrambling to build new *business* and *organization capabilities* in the hope of capitalizing on emerging opportunities.

Business capabilities are "what" the company needs to be able to do to execute its business strategy (e.g., support customers through any medium — phone, fax, Web, etc.). These capabilities are operational in nature and determine what results are desired. Organization capabilities are "how" the organization achieves its business capabilities (e.g., how it makes decisions and collaborates across boundaries). These capabilities need to exist throughout every aspect of the business. They create competitive advantage by building the capabilities that employees desire, customers love, and competitors can't copy.

No longer can a few good leaders be expected to propagate desired capabilities through vision, attributes, and communication alone. Capability development requires aligned and orchestrated action. Capabilities must be built fast and be adaptable to changing conditions.

Here's what this means for:

...an alternative fuel-cell manufacturer defining a new market space. The ability to:

- deliver a clean application of new technology for commercial use
- assemble core "Product Sets" that are readily adaptable to client needs and can be deployed rapidly and operated cost-effectively
- partner with other fuel-cell players in the original equipment manufacturer (OEM) network

...a regional utility company learning to thrive in a deregulated environment. The capacity to:

- manage the business in a deregulated environment vs. managing costs in a price-regulated market
- prioritize opportunities for financing (more opportunities than money available)
- incubate new services and spin them off

...a successful call-center company wishing to capitalize on the new dynamics of customer relationship management brought about by e-commerce. The ability to:

- integrate the full spectrum of voice and Internet communications, including custom e-mail response, "chat," and extensive web co-browsing capabilities
- provide Business to Business (B2B) electronic channel and database management and help companies inform, acquire, service, grow, and retain their customers throughout the entire relationship life cycle
- manage client contracts and relationships for full "Life-Cycle Profitability"

...an electronic manufacturing services firm moving up the supply chain. The capability to:

- shift from a site-centric model where site profit and loss (P&L) rules to a total-customer-solutions world where the whole is greater than the sum of its parts
- acquire and assimilate new design and service capabilities
- present one face to the customer and roll up profits by customer

The Greeks had a word that captures a juncture in time when opportunities and challenges meet and, if accepted, lead to new greatness and excellence. The word is "Kairos."

Kairos Moments

Defining the E-CRM (Customer Relationship Management) World

Ken Tuchman, CEO of TeleTech Holdings, had a history of anticipating unfilled niches. As a teenager in California he began importing puka shells that were used in necklaces for surfers. These necklaces later became a popular women's fashion, and Ken was a major supplier to J. C. Penney and other retailers. Years later, as a partner in a real-estate firm that specialized in building custom homes for the "rich and famous," he noticed a missing link between direct advertising and potential customers. As a customer dealing with the manufacturers, he experienced a glaring need for open, real-time lines of communication with customers. So in 1982 he founded TeleTech, to provide call-center services at a service level the companies themselves couldn't match.

After returning from a client call in the winter of 1998, Ken realized that TeleTech faced a Kairos moment. The company had grown from having a revenue of $1 million in its first year to well on the way to over $400 million. Although TeleTech had built world-class capabilities in rapidly deploying call centers anywhere in the world, this was not good enough for the customer interaction centers Ken saw so clearly ahead. Sitting in his corner office in Denver's Lincoln Center, Tuchman articulated his vision in a communication to all employees. During the next five years, TeleTech would become the only company to provide the range of technology-enabled products and services, content, and solutions that would allow companies to effectively manage the entire spectrum of customer relationships for competitive advantage. Furthermore, TeleTech would deploy these capabilities throughout the Global 1000. This broad installation would position TeleTech to deliver end-to-end customer relationship management solutions for a growing customer base. The client's end-to-end customer relationship management solutions would revolutionize the manner in which companies compete, and would revolutionize the consumer's experience with those companies.

In the 18-month period that followed, TeleTech put this vision into action by rigorously and rapidly building business and organization capabilities. The result? Not only did TeleTech grab the outsourced e-CRM market, reaching nearly $1 billion in sales in 2001; it also was in position to provide its multi-channel e-CRM technology platform capabilities to the in-source marketplace through an Application Service Provider (ASP) offering.

The Race for Alternate Fuel Technology

As fuel prices continued to rise in 2000, the big automobile manufacturers accelerated their interest in alternate fuels such as propane, natural gas, and hydrogen. Syed Hussein, a former commander in the Pakistan army, knew he needed a quick strike. His company, Quantum Technologies, had developed core competencies in fuel-cell technology, but now had to make it financially viable by meeting the demands of automobile production schedules and developing stationary power.

Syed delivered this vision to his senior team at a management meeting in Newport Beach. The team spent the rest of the day defining the business capabilities they would need and the processes to deliver those capabilities. Following the meeting, the team all piled into a bus. On the way to dinner, Syed reflected on the day. From the back of the bus, he summarized the challenge: "It's the poor execution (of strategy) that kills companies, not the strategy itself."

Already key OEMs were placing demands on his organization that they couldn't meet. Quantum Technologies was facing a Kairos moment.

While smaller, upstart companies must continually reshape themselves for survival, what about larger, more mature companies?

Navigating New Horizons

To signify the important changes ahead for StorageTek, the hall for the company's annual leadership conference was decked out in a nautical theme: "Navigating to New Horizons." StorageTek had a 30-year history, with its share of successes in the tape-storage market, but had recently run into problems as it tried to redirect its energies around its customers' need for storage solutions.

CEO Pat Martin stood alone on the deck of the ship. He knew he had the talent and solutions that provided a compelling picture of storage experts. That wasn't his major concern. Addressing the company's top 150 leaders, he summarized the company's Kairos moment.

While he would like a great strategy, he'd accept a good, consistent strategy that was consistently executed. It was not storage networking or global services technical capabilities that would blow them off course – it was the organization's discipline around a shared mindset, speed of change, accountability, and collaboration that would determine its success.

Later in the conference, the leadership team ceremoniously placed images of the company viruses that lie at the heart of its resistance to change into a hazardous waste container. Pat knew that identifying the viruses was only the first part of eliminating them. Now the hard, disciplined work of building organization capability was about to begin.

Pat needed more leaders on the deck with him to reach the new horizon.

Building the Nimble, 800-Pound Gorilla (General Electric)[1]

Valued as the largest company in the world, General Electric (GE) is known as an organization that gets results by responding quickly to change. It could be argued that Jack

Welch's legacy will be that he was the chief architect of a company and group of leaders that mastered the process of deploying global capabilities on an ongoing basis.

The GE story is well known: the series of divestitures and acquisitions made to be Number 1 (or 2) in the industry, the building of GE Capital into a financial services powerhouse, and exploiting the opportunities of e-commerce.

Throughout these Kairos moments GE demonstrated a disciplined approach to building capabilities and the employee commitment behind it.

GE's famed town meetings and Work-Out programs crashed through organizational boundaries and helped promote a boundaryless view of the enterprise. These programs not only solved short-term problems caused by bureaucracy, they accelerated GE's capability to deploy products and services globally at the same time. Later GE's Six Sigma program rooted out the cause of defects in existing business processes and laid the groundwork for designing new processes that would deliver new capabilities – at a quality level and speed that couldn't be readily matched. Adding to the Six Sigma knowledge-base and the common language it promoted were efforts to consolidate backroom environments. Not just a cost-savings program, these experiences and the knowledge gained put GE in a position to exploit the B2B e-commerce landscape.

Clearly not "flavor-of-the-month programs," these initiatives were actively championed by the companies' leaders and provided the building blocks for competitive advantage.

These Kairos moments reveal three fundamental lessons about successfully meeting challenges:

1　Leaders need to be focused on vision and making that vision actionable.
2　Leadership is more than the CEO; it takes a "village of leaders" to build capabilities.
3　A capability focus (the business and technical things companies need to do *and* how they execute them) turns out to be the Rosetta Stone in unlocking the organization's potential.

In the remainder of this chapter, we provide a quick, broad-brush overview of a repeatable process to build competitive advantage.

The Anatomy of the Capable Company[2]

Successful implementation of strategies requires both communication and solid project execution and fundamental changes in the behavior of the existing organization and its business processes. This includes all the functions, people, technology, workflows, policies, procedures, and performance-management systems and the way these interact to carry on an existing or new business process. Each organization has its own culture, including an inherent ability to resist change. As savvy leaders know, these elements interrelate in extraordinary complex and subtle ways.

Time and time again organizations face two major dilemmas that often undermine successful strategy execution. Top-level executives often fail to define focus and align the actions necessary to fully execute business transformation.

The other dilemma stems from the fundamental difference between the nature of a new business strategy and business-as-usual, day-to-day operations. Because business strategies and capabilities embrace multiple functions, the operating changes that must be implemented involve the organization as a whole as well as its components. Successful execution of strategy requires an integrated, systematic approach to build capabilities. However, because day-to-day activities are considered "must-do" they generally take precedence over any efforts associated with new strategies. Consequently the strategic work can become derailed or postponed all too easily. Even when there is a strong, widely shared commitment to build required capabilities, good intentions can quickly fade and implementation break down as normal day-to-day pressures and crises cause individuals to shift their priorities and diffuse their efforts.

As Steve Kerr, Chief Learning Officer at Goldman Sachs, says: "companies merrily go about hoping for A while rewarding B."

Identifying Vision Is Only Half the Job

At its core, strategic planning is a process that documents a set of choices made by the leadership team of a business. It describes the vision, objectives, goals, and supporting action plans, along with the rationale and implications associated with these choices. However, as companies seek to realize a new vision, the momentum for change often stalls when leadership lacks a disciplined approach to orchestrate change within their organizations.

To realize vision, leadership must be concerned with three key priorities that we believe lie at the heart of the Capable Company:

1   Developing a set of Business Capabilities to capitalize on the vision.
2   Translating Business Capability requirements into business processes, technologies, and organization.
3   Deploying a process for rapid, ongoing realignment of key process, technology, and organization elements.

As straightforward as this may sound, most company efforts aimed at their vision are off the mark. Interviews with over 100 executives reveal several common root causes leading to strategy execution failure:

- Rapid changes in technology and business process require a consistent disciplined approach, yet most companies don't have a consistent enterprise-wide strategy.
- Incorrect decisions are made because current reality fails to take into account predictable future events.
- Companies are constrained in the execution of their business plan by past business application choices.
- Key initiatives are often launched from functional silos, lacking alignment and fit with the greater organization with respect to process, technology, and/or organization.
- Financial planning and budgeting fail to take into account the timing and interaction between projects.

The consequences can be disastrous, as we can see in table 1.1, which depicts IT to business alignment problems.

To address these issues, companies need a breakthrough approach for rapidly realizing the new business capabilities dictated by the vision, strategy,

Table 1.1   Lessons Learned from Other Companies

	Situation	*Assessment*
Dell	Abandoned its SAP implementation after investing over $20 m in the project.	Management realized late in the game that the system being implemented would not fit its new, decentralized management model that was believed to be a key source of competitive advantage.
Dow	Spent 7 years and $0.5 bn on implementing a mainframe-based enterprise system. Abandoned the project and started over with a client-server version.	The project duration exceeded the rate of technological change by such a degree that the system was obsolete before deployment. By anticipating that technology changes would in some way impact the project, management may well have adopted a different approach to bringing desired business capabilities to the organization.
Applied Materials	Abandoned its ERP project in mid-implementation.	The company found itself overwhelmed by the organizational changes caused by the project.

Source: Tom Davenport, "Putting the Enterprise into the Enterprise System," *Harvard Business Review,* July–August 1998.

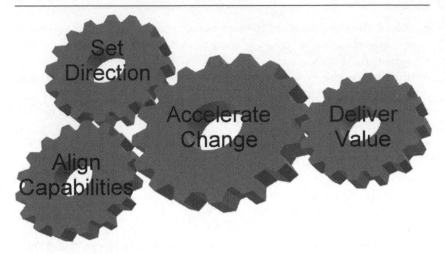

Figure 1.1   Capabilities that Make Strategy Work

and/or the change forces acting upon the business, whether it be techno-logical change, industry restructuring, deregulation, new customer needs, or competitive threats.

Our work with companies like Ford, StorageTek, Solectron, Blyth, GE, TeleTech, Viacom, and others suggest there are four major organization gears (see figure 1.1) that need to be interconnected and aligned to move the organization forward.

Setting Direction

As John Updike said in *Rabbit Run*, "If you don't know where you are headed, any road will get you there." Capable Companies excel at setting direction; the gear that sets in motion a series of actions and activities aimed at delivering value and trust in an ever-changing marketplace.

As a prerequisite to setting direction, Capable Companies have *and* develop great leaders. These leaders focus on the right results delivered in the right way, selflessly drive the vision to action, generate intellectual capital, and build organization capabilities – creating their own leadership brand. Leaders in Capable Companies don't dodge issues related to strategy deployment and systems alignment – they recognize these issues as essential leadership respon-sibilities and hold themselves accountable. They also create forums to work issues that cut across organization, process, and technology lines.

Capable Companies and their leaders provide the inspiration, direction, guidance, and boundaries for the company's journey. Through a disciplined process of clarifying purpose, mission, vision, and strategy they chart their course, and determine required capabilities to move on course while rapidly adjusting to changing conditions. They also relentlessly drive strategy to action. To make strategy real, Capable Companies articulate it in operational terms, such as the work that creates advantage in the eyes of the customer and other work that is intended to drive out inefficiencies. Finally, Capable Companies recognize that the key to success lies in the less glamorous development of business capabilities (what the business needs to do) and organization capabilities (how its management system operates).

Delivering Value

Strategy tells you who your most valuable customers are. Capable Companies create unique business focus and value propositions to those customers. According to Dave Ulrich, Jack Zenger, and Norm Smallwood, value propositions turn a company's attention outward. Understanding the primary value proposition (e.g., price, quality, speed, service, or innovation) helps target capabilities that create distinctiveness in the eyes of the customer. Capable Companies exploit the value exchange by determining the right products and services, then assuring the capability to deliver them. Increasingly, attention is paid to balancing infrastructure and superstructure; including creating alignment across customer and supplier boundaries to deliver value.

Capable Companies not only acquire customers; they know how to hold onto them and leverage new opportunities from them. They rigorously map needs and expectations to engagement methods, mine opportunities, and provide exceptional customer service, regardless of how valued customers come into contact with the company.

The Development and Alignment of Capabilities

With strategy set and value exchange mechanisms designed, the hard work of creating a dynamic business architecture begins; one that can adapt and shed, balance adaptive vs. disruptive technologies, and minimize organization and technical complexity. In Capable Companies, the job doesn't stop there. They align financial management, strategic planning processes, and IT to business needs. They also link performance management to desired results. We contend that the corporation's enabling systems are the key physical manifestation of its culture.

Capable Companies also understand the implications of various business archetypes on business architecture. For example, whether your corporate strategy seeks a high degree of synergy among its businesses or firewalls between them matters to capability development. Based on the choice made, certain capabilities fit better than others. Having a framework helps to identify early in the game the red flags that should be raised and the warning signals that should sound when trying to put a square peg in a round hole.

Accelerate Change

Capable Companies keep track of how they are doing through *balanced scorecards* that translate strategy into measurable terms. Since purpose, mission, and vision are longer-term in nature, scorecards have a core set of stable measures that track progress. Measurement systems must also be adaptable to changes in the marketplace that require new goals or new emphasis at any point in time. Capable Companies have figured out how to track key lead indicators that point to future targets and have aligned measures and feedback to the organization level and timing of required decisions.

To analyze and respond to constant environmental change, Capable Companies maintain a lightweight and highly effective planning process that:

- establishes a rapid-response mechanism for monitoring and responding to external and internal change forces;
- identifies the essential business and organization capabilities required to achieve enterprise goals;
- aligns business process, technology, and organizational strategies to improve operational capability;
- evaluates potential actions against architectural constraints;
- calibrates the measurement system as needed;
- defines and prioritizes critical initiatives;
- deploys an ongoing, rapid (e.g., three-month) program and project integration cycle.

Returning to our gear metaphor, this process provides the enterprise with insight to either accelerate or apply the brakes in response to changing conditions.

Just How Capable Is Your Company?

Take the quiz in table 1.2 to see how capable your company is.

Table 1.2 The Capable Company Self-Assessment

	Circle	One
1. Your top management is focused, aligned, results-oriented and relentlessly drives vision to action.	Yes	No
2. Your company has determined business capabilities for delivering the value proposition.	Yes	No
3. Your company has the ability to jump from one course to another while maintaining some headway toward a set of goals.	Yes	No
4. To maximize value to investors, your company strives for the least long-term debt/capital *and* maximizes appreciable assets (knowledge capital).	Yes	No
5. Your company has one face to the customer and can guarantee the experience regardless of the method of customer interaction, even when multiple partners are involved.	Yes	No
6. Your company has a business architecture that can assess trade-offs in people, process, and technology.	Yes	No
7. Your HR systems, financial systems, and IT strategies fully support your business strategy.	Yes	No
8. You have a corporate scorecard that tracks your strategy, is balanced between financial and non-financial measures, and is deployed throughout the enterprise.	Yes	No
9. Key projects really do get the results they tout.	Yes	No
10. Your company routinely monitors change forces and has a process for rapid, ongoing realignment of key process, technology, and organizational elements.	Yes	No

The Tally

If you answered yes to all the questions your company has figured out the synergy between people, process, and technology and you have created a company that is capable of executing strategy.

If you answered yes to 7–9 questions you are probably running at a competitive advantage and may only need to tweak your business architecture.

If you answered yes to only 4–6 questions there is hope for the road ahead, but attention to critical capabilities is required or opportunities may be squandered.

If you answered yes to 3 or fewer questions, your company is living in the past and may be in deep trouble.

Summary

Poor strategy is often the scapegoat when companies' performance suffers. It is more often a case of bad execution. While most company leaders are trying to do the right thing, they're not aligned or equipped to execute the game plan.

This chapter provided a broad-brush overview of the concepts for building capabilities that make strategy work and outlined our four-part approach to the book – symbolized by interlocking and aligned gears.

Subsequent chapters address specific components and tools that help leaders at all levels build and diffuse capabilities to better execute their strategy.

Notes

1   Rich Lynch, who was part of the Six Sigma consulting team at GE Capital from 1996 to 1998, made these observations.
2   Adapted from Richard Lynch and Kelvin Cross, *Measure Up: How to Measure Corporate Performance* (Blackwell Business, 1995).

Part I Setting Direction

Strategy without tactics is the slowest route to victory. Tactics without strategy is the noise before defeat.

– Sun Tzu

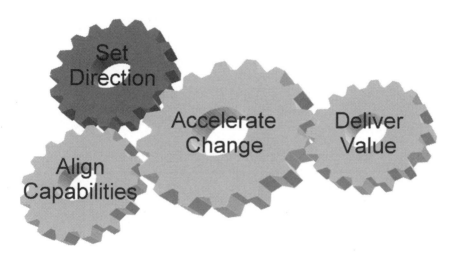

2 Enable Capable Leaders

Good business leaders create a Vision, articulate the Vision, passionately own the Vision, and relentlessly drive it to completion.

— **Jack Welch**

The Purpose of This Chapter

While strategic vision is the job of a select few, strategy execution is the responsibility of many. Once direction is set and the company gears are put in motion to achieve a set of desired results, leaders at every level must focus on strategy alignment and execution. This chapter provides a snapshot of leadership performance: what it means to be results-focused and how to build capability to respond quickly to an uncertain future. Key to this success is generating intellectual capital in the company and purposefully building leadership bench strength.

Capable Companies must have capable leaders. But what makes a capable leader? To paraphrase Warren Bennis:

1   Leaders find staying with the "status quo" unacceptable.
2   Leaders have the ability to create a social architecture capable of generating intellectual capital.
3   Leaders give followers direction, trust, and hope.[1]

In short, leaders provide opportunities to stakeholders by creating the capabilities that deliver on a promise.

When that direction falters or trust is broken, the results can be devastating, as witnessed in the high-profile falls of Worldcom, Enron, Aldelpia, Cendant, and Tyco. In these cases top executives behaved more like rock stars: "I deserve huge compensation . . . the rules don't apply to me . . . I'm bigger than life." Results mattered, but how they got them didn't.

While companies scramble to revisit their code of ethics, the real challenge is making that code real to the organization. As Kenneth Goodman, co-director of the ethics programs at the University of Miami, puts it:

> You have to send the message from the top and weave this into corporate development. It's professional development . . . how do you make the tough calls? It's not all about virtue, it's about critical thinking.[2]

The Challenges

Getting the right results matters. Top executives and human resources professionals are addressing how those results are achieved – now and in the future.

Ironically, for much of the past 50 years, leadership development has focused on the personal traits of executives and their leadership styles, whether that leader was on the battlefield or in the boardroom. Trait theory evolved to codify leadership competencies and styles around people and tasks. Kenneth Blanchard added to the body of work by introducing "situational leadership," a concept focused on adapting leadership behaviors to various employee situations (you manage a newcomer differently from a veteran). In the 1990s, Steve Covey's universal principles, found in *7 Habits of Effective People*, became the focus of management retreats. More recently, leadership literature focuses on hero stories behind great CEOs like GE's Jack Welch and Southwest Airlines' Herb Kelleher.

Yet with all the dollars spent on leadership competencies and behaviors, companies have a tough time measuring the payback in terms of building value and trust.

We believe that its time to move beyond a competency-only focus. The following challenges that keep many executives awake at night need to be addressed in a new way:

1   Getting the right results.
2   Driving the agenda.
3   Generating intellectual capital.
4   Accelerating the development of leaders.
5   Relentlessly focusing on execution.

Getting the Right Results in the Right Way

The "Leadership = Results" School

To paraphrase the Beatles' parting words of wisdom on *Abbey Road*: "and in the end the results you take are equal to the results you make." It not just the high-profile accounting-scandal cases that apply here. Judging from the turnaround at the top of many companies, the right results have come up short too many times. Challenger, Gray, & Christmas, an international outplacement firm, noted from August 1999 to July 2000 that 1,151 top executives were forced out of their jobs, resigned voluntarily, or retired. There were 129 CEO departures in October 2000 alone, up 115 percent from the previous year. Of those resignations the largest percentage "resigned" (34 percent) and another 5 percent were "fired, ousted or replaced."

"Months on the job, not just years, may be the measure of performance. There is no hesitation by directors to ask a CEO to leave if there is even the slightest hint that numbers will not be met," according to John A. Challenger, CEO at Challenger, Gray & Christmas. Warren Buffet's action at Gillette in the fall of 2000 is a case in point. After succeeding Al Zeien, who led Gillette's golden era of the Sensor and Mach3 products, as well as the acquisition of Duracell, Michael C. Hawley lasted only 18 months at the helm. Although comfortable with Gillette's strategy, Buffet and fellow board members did not have confidence in Hawley at the execution level.[3]

Yet execution does not mean "earnings at any cost" that lead to a loss of faith by customers, employees, and investors.

The "Leadership = Attributes" School

Leadership development in many companies has focused on identifying characteristics of admired leaders and investing in building these characteristics for a select few "high potentials." The problem with this approach is threefold. First, leadership development is generic across companies (everyone trying to build the same set of competencies). Second, they focus only on leadership behaviors. Third, they are not linked to the desired results.

In short, both schools of leadership are only half right.

The approach to leadership has to encompass both what results are desired and how these results are delivered, so that leaders stand for something. When this happens companies build value and earn trust.

Linking Attributes to Results

Results-Based Leadership, Inc. has taken leadership theory an important step forward by linking attributes (knowledge, skills, and/or traits) to desired business results. In their landmark book, *Results-Based Leadership,*[4] authors Ulrich, Zenger, and Smallwood challenge the conventional wisdom surrounding leadership. They argue that it is not enough to gauge leaders by personal traits such as character, style, and values. Many of the leaders "ousted" from their jobs were renowned for their personal character and integrity. Effective leaders know how to connect leadership *attributes* with desired *results,* as shown in figure 2.1.

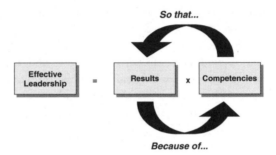

Figure 2.1   The Formula for Effective Leadership
Source: Results-Based Leadership, Inc.

For example, the attributes from a regional utility company shown in table 2.1 are more powerful when linked to results.

The relationship of attributes and results is multiplicative, not additive.

According to Smallwood, leaders who get results but have weak leadership attributes (how they get the results) are less likely to repeat performance. "Chainsaw Al" Dunlop is a case in point. While he did achieve short-term financial results by slashing the Sunbeam organization, he did nothing to foster the development of the leaders needed to create the capabilities for long-term success. Conversely, leaders with high attribute scores independent of results are like golfers who have a great knowledge of the game and technique but can't break 100. Eastman Kodak's former CEO Kay Whitmore falls into this category. Well known throughout Kodak for his personal integrity, he could not mobilize Kodak fast enough to move into the digital imaging world.[5]

Capable Companies work with leaders *at all levels* to develop the desired capabilities that enable them to execute better today and to build a foundation

Table 2.1 The Attributes–Results Connection

These attributes of leaders	Result in	To the benefit of
Take a strategic perspective	Outperforming the competition by moving into profitable power-generation business and improving EPS.	Investor
Exhibit speed and agility	Adapting sooner and more effectively than the competition to changes and introducing new products in shorter time-spans in a deregulated environment.	Customer
Align the organization	Everyone can be held accountable for actions and projects that contribute more effectively to the execution of the corporate, "allied" strategy.	Organization
Energize and empower others	Retaining talent that is more likely to remain committed to the future of the organization.	Employee and the organization

to deliver what they have promised to do in the future. Leaders who know what results to deliver, as well as how to deliver them consistent with firm values, increase confidence among employees, customers, and investors.

Driving the Agenda

Since strategy articulates value promised in the future, leaders are responsible for translating strategy into clear actions that provide direction. Strategy doesn't just happen. Strategy can't be inferred; the capabilities to execute it must be mapped out.

At TeleTech, the vision to revolutionize the e-CRM space meant creating a new kind of customer-interaction center. To drive home his point, CEO Ken Tuchman symbolically fined managers for using the old term "call center." Tuchman drove the agenda by first defining the capabilities needed for his visionary customer interaction center and then examined old, new, and potential projects and how they would contribute to the building of those capabilities.

In figure 2.2, projects are shown in the building blocks and the capabilities are portrayed as the layers. For TeleTech, key projects were needed to keep the business moving forward (contributing to the mission), while other projects were carefully sequenced to provide new opportunities.

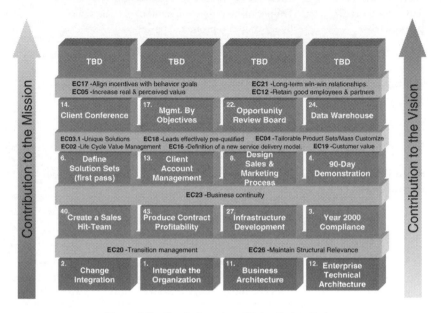

Figure 2.2   Key Projects in a 90-day Review Cycle

In figure 2.2, the shading of the mission and vision arrows refers to relative contribution; e.g., high contribution to the mission in the beginning. TeleTech identified 26 Enterprise Capabilities (i.e., leverage points to help move the company in the direction of the vision). By sorting Capabilities to support their mission (how the enterprise must do business) and those that support their vision (shared image of what the enterprise wants to become), clarity was brought to the difference between the two and the necessity to coexist.

Ranking some 40 projects according to their value and assessing execution risk focused executive attention. For example, if a project had a high contribution to the mission and low volatility (e.g., technology is stable), it made the list.

The first row of projects represents the "footings" and provides the capabilities of "transition management" and "structural relevance" shown as mortar.

The next row of foundation bricks represents the projects needed to ensure business continuity – essential to the mission.

As you go up the chart, the projects start to contribute more to the vision.

In essence, the TeleTech team filtered investment decisions as to whether the project could be invested in stages, provided additional flexibility when combined with other projects, or generated new growth opportunities. As illustrated in table 2.2, this allowed them the option of reacting to future opportunities.

Table 2.2 Sequencing Projects

Project	Option Type	Investment Plan	Impact
1. Enterprise technical architecture	**Staging**	Invest now	Technical Architecture viewed as critical input to determining the sequencing of IT investments and make/buy/lease decisions.
2. "90-day product demo"	**Growth**	Invest now	This pilot, designed to demonstrate synergies between proprietary technologies, will be used to sell clients on the potential of the product platform.
3. Define product solution modules	**Flexibility**	Maybe now	This move to modular product design, away from custom development, will support solution re-use and rapid deployment. *Evaluate resources after "Invest Nows" are launched.*
4. Client account management	**Growth**	Probably later	Prerequisite projects and change management efforts must be accomplished before this project can be successfully implemented. *Take a wait-and-see approach, but be ready to act.*
5. Implement Oracle human resource module	**Staging**	Maybe later	Despite the momentum behind the Oracle implementation in other areas, this did not immediately support required critical capabilities. *Revisit in 6 months.*

Key
Staging – invest in stages rather than all at once, allowing decisions (new options) at critical stages.
Growth – investment creates future growth options above and beyond the returns generated by the initial investment.
Flexibility – investments generate interaction and provide options not previously possible.

Using this approach, TeleTech progressed toward the creation of customer-interaction centers, but maintained the flexibility to shift gears as technology evolved and as customer requirements changed. For example, as some customers sought to run their own customer-interaction centers, TeleTech was in a position to move its product set over to an application software provider platform – allowing TeleTech to corner both the outsource and the in-source markets.

> **The trick for leaders in setting direction is making the next landfall and not preventing future options.**

Generating Intellectual Capital

In today's boundaryless organization and federated structures, intellectual capital[6] must be harnessed from and shared throughout the extended enterprise that includes alliance partners, suppliers, and customers. According to James Brian Quinn:

> The capacity to manage human intellect – and to convert it into useful products and services – is fast becoming the critical executive skill of the age.[7]

This presents three challenges for leaders. First, they must continuously hire the best professionals. Although much maligned in the late 1980s for their product-out mentality, Wang Laboratories' earlier rise to success was based on Dr. Wang's recruitment of Harold Koplow, a pharmacist who led the software development revolution with the practical introduction of word processing and related products. Second, leaders must break down the barriers that lock knowledge in pockets of the organization. Again Wang is a case in point – this time for the failure to meet this challenge. In 1982, Koplow had essentially designed a network of PCs with a graphical user interface – two years before the Macintosh. This time Wang stumbled and squandered this new knowledge by breaking up the concept and barricading the components in the existing structure: networks, Central Processing Unit (CPU), and workstations. Koplow resigned and Wang began its slow, painful freefall. Third, leaders must *lead* in the development of the systems to capture knowledge from disaggregated structures. Today's emphasis on enterprise-guidance systems is a case in point. Given the explosion of Customer Relationship Management (CRM) and Enterprise Resource Planning (ERP), there is a plethora of data, but these systems provide mostly functional feedback and not the strategic enterprise insight needed for meaningful review and actions.

Hiring and Leveraging Professional Intellect

According to Quinn, managing human intellect resembles coaching more than anything else: recruit the best based on the set of skills demanded by the strategy and the capability gaps that exist, force intensity and early development, constantly raise the bar, and objectively evaluate and weed out non-performers.[8] GE is a case in point. Known for hiring the best and the brightest and putting them through a rigorous course of training and assignments, they continually s–t–r–e–t–c–h employees to exceed goals. Welch constantly set the bar higher, as he rightly knew that otherwise, it is impossible to find out what people can do.[9] GE also does the tough, detailed performance management work by routinely weeding out the bottom 10 percent.

Analog Devices, Inc. is another company that stretches its human capital by leveraging process knowledge. First, the company set half-life goals for leaders and improvement teams. One half-life is the estimated time in months it takes to cut a defect rate in half, based on the organizational and technical complexity of the problem and the theoretical limits of the process.[10] Analog Devices relentlessly applied quality-improvement techniques and shared process-improvement experiences related to the goal. When the half-life approach was originally introduced in the late 1980s, wafer-fabrication yields were in the 20–30 percent range and a 50 percent yield was thought impossible. By applying the half-life goals and focused improvement team projects on the problem, yields reached the 50 percent marker in just a few years, delaying the costly development of a new wafer-fabrication facility and giving Analog the option of waiting for emerging technology to stabilize.

Removing the Barriers

GE's "Work-Out" and its cousin ACT at IBM are heralded techniques to help break down the organizational boundaries that prevent knowledge from flowing freely in companies. Knowledge needs to flow freely in problem solving and also in knowledge creation. To help identify barriers to knowledge flow, Ron Ashkenas, Dave Ulrich, Todd Jick, and Steve Kerr have categorized four types of boundaries: vertical, horizontal, external, and global, as shown in table 2.3.[11]

Ashkenas et al. have created a quick assessment of how your intellectual capital is managed and promulgated throughout the organization, reprinted here as table 2.4.

Table 2.3 Organization Boundaries

Vertical Boundary	The degree to which the organization chart, span of control, and approval levels slow knowledge sharing.
Horizontal Boundary	The degree to which functional silos prevent knowledge workers from creating value in core processes and sharing knowledge among core processes.
External Boundary	The degree to which existing structure and systems inhibit flow of ideas and information from customers and suppliers.
Global Boundary	The degree to which companies act locally without thinking globally.

Table 2.4 Stepping Up To the Line: How Boundaryless Is Your Organization?

Instructions: *The following 16 statements describe the behavior of boundaryless organizations. Assess the extent to which each statement characterizes your current organization, circling a number from 1 (not true at all) to 5 (very true).*

Boundary Type	Speed	Flexibility	Integration	Innovation	Total
Vertical	Most decisions are made on the spot by those closest to the work, and they are acted on in hours rather than weeks. 1 2 3 4 5	Managers at all levels routinely take on frontline responsibilities as well as broad strategic assignments. 1 2 3 4 5	Key problems are tracked by multilevel teams whose members operate with little regard to formal rank in the organization. 1 2 3 4 5	New ideas are screened and decided on without fancy overheads and multiple rounds of approvals. 1 2 3 4 5	
Horizontal	New products or services are getting to market at an increasingly fast pace. 1 2 3 4 5	Resources quickly, frequently, and effortlessly shift between centers of expertise and operating units. 1 2 3 4 5	Routine work gets done through end-to-end process teams: project teams drawn from shared centers of experience handle other work. 1 2 3 4 5	Ad hoc teams representing various stakeholders spontaneously to explore new ideas. 1 2 3 4 5	
External	Customer requests, complaints, and needs are anticipated and responded to in real time. 1 2 3 4 5	Strategic resources and key managers are often "on loan" to customers and suppliers. 1 2 3 4 5	Supplier and customer reps are key players in teams tackling strategic initiatives. 1 2 3 4 5	Suppliers and customers are regular and prolific contributors of new product and process ideas. 1 2 3 4 5	
Global	Best practices are disseminated and leveraged quickly across country operations. 1 2 3 4 5	Business leaders rotate regularly between country operations. 1 2 3 4 5	There are standard product platforms, common practices, and shared centers of experience across companies. 1 2 3 4 5	New product ideas are evaluated for viability beyond the country where they emerged. 1 2 3 4 5	
Total					

Scoring: Sum the rows and columns. Rows represent the permeability of your boundaries. A score of 12 or less in a row indicates an area for improvement. Columns represent your organization's achievement in a key success area. Again, a score of 12 or less indicates an area for improvement.

Knowledge-Management Systems (KMS)

As companies get larger, the need for knowledge transfer is greater. Capable Companies invest in Knowledge-Management Systems to get the most from their human capital.[12] With external computerized databases, many companies are creating repositories of internally sourced and structured knowledge for applications such as product knowledge, marketing knowledge, and customer knowledge.[13]

Managing the intellectual capital in the new products phase can have huge results. James Brian Quinn observes: "the intangibles that add value to most products and services are knowledge-based: technical know-how, product design, marketing presentation, understanding the customer, personal creativity, and innovation."[14]

Accelerating the Development of Leaders

In the fall of 1999, analysts gathered at GE to get a glimpse of the unthinkable: GE *after* Jack Welch. During the session analysts got a rare look into how GE develops executives. At the conclusion of the meeting, they left knowing "the supremacy of ideas over individuals was at the core of GE's success – and concern diminished about the ability of leaders at GE to continue to drive results in the post-Welch GE era."[15] In fact, not only did GE stock hold its own in December 2000 when Welch eventually named his successor, Jeffrey Immelt from GE Medical Systems, but the runners-up for the post who decided to leave GE had an instant, positive impact on their new companies in an otherwise flat market.

Table 2.5 GE Executives' Impact on New Companies

GE Executive	New Company	Stock Impact
James McInerney, former head of GE Aircraft Engines	3M	Stock moved 11% on the news that day and 17% by the week's end.
Robert Nardelli, GE Power Systems	Home Depot	Stock rose 10% on the news that day. A month later, it was up over 22%.

The premium price in the market that GE leadership commands is what Ulrich, Smallwood, and Zenger have coined *leadership brand*.[16]

Brand represents delivery on a promise to the stakeholders of the company. Like product brand (e.g., Coke, Mach 3) or company brand (e.g., Nordstrom's, Dell Computer Corporation, Disney), leadership brand also means differentiation in the intangibles of the company and the perception of future earnings.

Whether a company articulates its leadership brand in a formal statement or not, most insiders know what it is. The benefits of formalizing a leadership brand statement include:

- Allowing for both unity and diversity – SBU/department/core process deviations for local diversity are based on a common understanding of corporate intent.
- Setting expectations for leadership results *and* leadership attributes for leaders at every level and in every business, function, and team.
- Ensuring individual initiatives have consistent goals – everyone knows what is expected and how to develop greater capability to do it.
- Providing direction to leadership development – training and development needs, what kind of learning is most important, what results are highest priority, what pieces could be integrated for greater impact, etc.

Jack Welch – The Ultimate Leadership Brand Manager
GE is certainly known as an organization that gets results and responds quickly to change. Beneath the GE mantra of "speed, simplicity, and self-confidence" is a well-oiled machine that delivers results.

Key attributes of leaders reinforced through hiring, rewards, promotion, and training:

- Have external awareness.
- Build organizational talent.
- Build collaborative relationships.
- Have financial understanding and focus.
- Hold people accountable.
- Lead change.

Process for leadership development:

- Strong recruiting program.
- Extensive use of job-rotation assignments.
- Crotonville Executive Development campus.
- Common language through Six Sigma.

Continued

- Green Belt for Champions and Process Management (Six Sigma).
- Change Acceleration Process training.

Accountability through measurements:

- Open-book approach to financials.
- Strong culture to be measured by financial results.
- Process management accountability.
- Non-financial results emphasized through Six Sigma.
- "Dashboards" for company, core process, and enabling processes.

Leadership culture that delivers results:

- Strong culture to be measured by financial results.
- Only top performers make it.
- Be number 1 or 2 in markets in which they compete.
- Pinnacle rewards for high achievers (not just sales).

The assessment in figure 2.3 can be used to evaluate your company's leadership brand.

Leaders also build intangible value by defining and creating organization capabilities. In their book, *Why the Bottom Line Isn't* (Wiley 2003), Ulrich and Smallwood propose that a hierarchy of intangibles exists:

- A consistent delivery of earnings quarter by quarter, year by year.
- A clear growth plan.
- Ensuring business capabilities are aligned to the strategy (the focus of this book).
- Creating organization capabilities (the focus of *Why the Bottom Line Isn't*, and touched upon in chapter 4 here).

A Relentless Focus on Execution

Like Gillette's removal of Michael C. Hawley, Compaq CEO Eckhard Pfeiffer wasn't removed because of a flawed strategy. It was something more mundane: poor execution.

Results		Criteria	Attributes	
Low	*High*		*Low*	*High*
To what extent has the strategy of the firm been expressed in specific desired results over the next 18 months? 1 2 3 4 5 6 7 8 9 10		**Strategic**	To what extent do leaders have attributes/competencies consistent with business priorities determined by the strategy? 1 2 3 4 5 6 7 8 9 10	
To what extent are results balanced across the four results areas — customer, investor, employee, organization? 1 2 3 4 5 6 7 8 9 10		**Balanced**	To what extent do we have a complete set of competencies that link to customer, investor, employee, and organization outcomes? 1 2 3 4 5 6 7 8 9 10	
To what extent are the expected results what we need to become, not what we have been? 1 2 3 4 5 6 7 8 9 10		**Long-Term/ Future**	To what extent do competency models focus on the future and what is next, not just past and present? 1 2 3 4 5 6 7 8 9 10	
To what extent are leaders successful in making the whole greater than the parts to drive total business results? 1 2 3 4 5 6 7 8 9 10		**Selfless**	To what extent do leaders demonstrate attributes that reflect the organization's key values and go beyond personal effectiveness to build team and organization capabilities? 1 2 3 4 5 6 7 8 9 10	
To what extent are results turned into vital signs that can be tracked differently for leaders at all levels? 1 2 3 4 5 6 7 8 9 10		**Operational**	To what extent are attributes put into measurable behavioral terms? 1 2 3 4 5 6 7 8 9 10	
To what extent do leaders at every level deliver results consistent with the overall strategy of the firm? 1 2 3 4 5 6 7 8 9 10		**Leaders at Every Level**	To what extent do leaders at different levels know how to develop attributes consistent with their desired results? 1 2 3 4 5 6 7 8 9 10	
To what extent do our people processes support desired results? 1 2 3 4 5 6 7 8 9 10			To what extent do our people processes enable leaders to develop appropriate attributes? 1 2 3 4 5 6 7 8 9 10	
To what extent do our information and enterprise guidance processes support desired results? 1 2 3 4 5 6 7 8 9 10		**Enabling Processes**	To what extent do our information and knowledge management processes enable leaders to develop appropriate attributes? 1 2 3 4 5 6 7 8 9 10	
To what extent do our money and resource allocation processes support desired results? 1 2 3 4 5 6 7 8 9 10			To what extent do our information and enterprise guidance processes enable leaders to develop appropriate attributes? 1 2 3 4 5 6 7 8 9 10	
To what extent do we convince outside stakeholders that we can improve and sustain results through our leaders? 1 2 3 4 5 6 7 8 9 10		**Reputation Management**	To what extent do our leaders model the organization's key leadership attributes and communicate their significance with outside stakeholders? 1 2 3 4 5 6 7 8 9 10	

Figure 2.3 Rating Your Company's Leadership Brand

1 Rate your organization on its current practices in each criterion on a scale of 1 to 10 by circling the appropriate number. Answer for both Attributes and Results.

2 Add the scores together for the 10 items for Results and write the sum in the Total Results Score. Add the scores together for Attributes and write the sum in the Total Attributes Score.

Scoring:
Add Results Scores: Total _____
Divide by 10
Average Results Score: _____

Scoring:
Add Attributes Scores: Total _____
Divide by 10
Average Attributes Score: _____

_____ x _____ = _____
Average Results Score   Average Attributes Score   Leadership Brand Score

To interpret your score, see below:

0–25: Tin Leaders
May have strong, charismatic individual leaders but there is not much in place to sustain results. Get to work!

26–50: Bronze Leaders
Good work has been done to set up basic systems and processes to develop individual leaders. Need to pull this all together to deliver sustained results. Investment in leadership alignment will have significant impact.

51–75: Silver Leaders
Most systems and processes for leadership development are integrated. Identify the few weak areas to move to next level. Focusing on the "right" areas is critical to get optimal bang for the leadership investment buck. Doing so will move you into the big leagues.

76–100: Gold Leaders
Mortgage the house and invest in this company. Results will be sustained. Analysts should be giving you a premium P:E multiple for your leadership brand.

Figure 2.3 Rating Your Company's Leadership Brand *Cont'd*

According to research on why CEOs fail, Ram Charan and Geoffrey Colvin claim:

> In the majority of cases – we estimate 70% – the real problem isn't the high-concept boners the boffins love to talk about. It's bad execution. As simple as that: not getting things done, being indecisive, not delivering on commitments.[17]

Different strategies can have effective results. Wang Labs, an early winner in the minicomputer race, was hauled over the coals for missing the PC revolution. The company could not muster alignment around a coherent strategy. Sun Microsystems, on the other hand, quietly executed its strategy to stay in the minicomputer or server game – ultimately emerging as one of the four horsemen of the Internet age, along with Cisco, EMC, and Oracle.

What Do Eight Out of Ten of Fortune's Most Admired Companies Have in Common?

In 1999, there was an interesting, unheralded common denominator of successful companies: eight of the ten companies on the most admired list had no Chief Operating Officer (COO). Or more to the point, their CEOs were bent on execution. From Jack Welch at GE to John Chambers at Cisco, to Michael Dell at Dell, to Southwest Airlines' Herb Kelleher, these leaders paid attention to critical initiatives and monitored their progress.

Michael Dell sums it up:

> Everyone has known about (our direct business model) for years. How can it be a competitive advantage? We execute it. It's all about knowledge and execution.

What do capable leaders do to help build Capable Companies? Here's our short-list:

- Monitor external and internal change forces

  As CBS continued to experience rapid growth through the acquisition and merger of traditional and new media properties, CEO Joe Seibert knew that, going forward, the relaxation of regulatory constraints would continue to provide significant growth opportunities, such as the merger with Viacom. He monitored other change forces such as distribution channel expansion, digital convergence, and e-commerce to bring added opportunities for growth. This growth places significant demand on the IT infrastructure and application system adaptability.

  Seibert also kept close watch on the competition – rivals in the same business and from other businesses vying for the same audiences. CBS observed that this trend would continue as increased bandwidth lowered barriers to entry, and made everyone a broadcaster in the same way that the Internet made everyone a publisher. The expanding number of available channels in traditional media, as well as the emergence of new media, e-commerce, and global distribution, is greatly increasing market segmentation and breaking all commerce paradigms.

  These trends are compelling media companies to produce, acquire, and distribute content more efficiently, to target content and advertising toward a more focused and individualized audience, and to compete in more of these narrow markets. New customer-engagement methods will place demands on the capabilities of the IT infrastructure to provide market agility, organizational flexibility, speed/time to market, and audience/consumer intimacy. This external review led Seibert to conclude that his IT infrastructure was not prepared to respond to these demands and rapidly put together a value-delivery plan to address the shortfalls.

- Identify key capabilities

  After many years of organic and acquisition-led growth a global hospitality company was underperforming. Its CEO initiated a program that decomposed the company into its fundamental chain of value-adding services. By sharpening focus on its set of Advantage-driving Capabilities, the company redesigned its structure and operating processes to deliver more value and drove out more than $100 million of cost.

- Denounce old capabilities no longer required

  Determining new capabilities is half the battle. De-emphasizing or undoing capabilities that are no longer needed is the other half. For example, at Quantum Technologies, Syed Hussein stressed the importance of undoing old habits such as current cost-accuracy capability in favor of customer quick response, and stopped rewarding salespeople for selling products when the customer was asking for a solution.

- Sponsor initiatives

  GE's Jack Welch sponsored just six major initiatives in his nearly 20 years as CEO: aim to be number 1 or 2; try to forge the boundaryless organization through "Work-Out"; 3S (speed, simplicity, and self-confidence); globalization; Six Sigma; and e-commerce.[18] Unlike many executives, who give lip service in annual reports, Welch walked the talk. From the mid-to late 1990s, Welch relentlessly drove Six Sigma throughout all GE's 12 businesses, focusing on GE Capital, its financial services profit engine, starting in the spring of 1996. By attending team report-outs, quizzing managers on their greenbelt projects, reviewing dashboards, etc., Welch exemplified the hands-on execution approach. Anyone who did not take it as seriously as him was in for a rough time. When one executive could not explain his greenbelt project during a review for a promotion, Welch immediately responded that he was not GE leadership material! This message was a shot heard around the GE world and enrollment at GE Capital's Greenbelt for Champions course skyrocketed.

- Keep track of critical assignments

  In undertaking a company-wide reengineering project, Peter Pyclik, Chief Operating Officer (COO) of an information services firm, established a transition team to lead the IT, process, and HR projects. Peter and the transition manager knew successful implementation would demand close coordination among the various projects and clear communications with operation management concerning strategies, schedules, and involvement. They also recognized that spending time on integration issues would build credibility! Integration issues (e.g., slow system performance, development of workstation standards, setting parameters and boundaries for support services, design change impacts on legal contracts, etc.) are complex from both an organizational and technical perspective. Constant vigilance over the multi-year project resulted in 20 percent across-the-board savings and successful transition from an intermediary to an infomediary, with the ability to handle much of the work over the Internet.

- Look for alignment issues and take decisive action when problems occur
  Dell Computer abandoned their ERP program only after several months of detail planning and implementation when they realized that is was inappropriate in their environment. The ERP solution certainly provided zero-latency data-availability, and it promised more seamless virtual integration and less complexity. However, other traits of the solution would have limited the ability of the company to manage processes in a distributed manner; violating the company's management and process improvement style.

- Monitor results
  Known for his work in building a Fortune 500 powerhouse in real-world signal processing, Analog Devices Chairman Ray Stata was also instrumental in forming the Center for Quality of Management (CQM) and carried out pioneering work on organizational learning. Through the CQM, he shared best practices among member companies, especially Analog's work on the balanced scorecard (see chapter 9). During the company's monthly operating meetings, Stata insisted that they begin with the Quality Improvement Process metrics, which covered customer service, new products, and manufacturing capability metrics before they turned their attention to the financials. In this way managers focused on the next quarter's results and shared learning on process improvement throughout the various divisions. In fact, Stata was more concerned with the rate of improvement than the actual measure.[19]

The Building Blocks of the Capable Company

- Capable Companies develop leaders who continuously align attributes and results. To do that, Capable Companies have competency models and scorecards and link the two.
- Capable leaders set direction for the next landfall without preventing future options. Two new skills are needed here: balancing the short-term and long-term view, and understanding the options presented in investment choices.
- Capable leaders pay close attention to the company's intellectual capital.
- Capable Companies articulate their Leadership Brand to provide direction for the training and development of their leaders, what kind of learning is most important, what results are highest priority and what pieces could be integrated for greater impact.
- Capable Companies build and measure intangible value.

> *Continued*
>
> • Capable Companies reward leaders who focus on execution. Leaders must spend adequate time on execution details, including business alignment issues, in order to minimize organization friction.

The following chapters zero in on the details of strategy execution.

Notes

1 Warren Bennis, *On Becoming a Leader* (Addison Wesley, 1994).
2 Marcia Heroux, "CEO search now factors in integrity," *Boston Globe*, August 4, 2002.
3 Chris Riley, "Acting Chief says Gillette to stay on current course, boost revenue," *Boston Globe*.
4 David Ulrich, Jack Zenger, and Norm Smallwood, *Results Based Leadership* (Harvard Business School Press, 1999).
5 Ram Charan and Geoffrey Colvin, "Why CEO's Fail," *Fortune*, June 21, 1999.
6 Larry Prusak of Ernst & Young defines intellectual capital as "the material that has been formalized, captured, and leveraged to produce a higher valued asset."
7 James Brian Quinn, Philip Anderson, and Sydney Finkelstein, "Making the most of the best," *Harvard Business School Review*, March–April 1996.
8 Ibid.
9 Robert Slater, *Jack Welch and the GE Way* (McGraw-Hill, 1999).
10 Arthur S. Schneiderman, "Setting Quality Goals," *Quality Progress*, April 1988.
11 Ron Ashkenas, Steve Kerr, Todd Jick, and Dave Ulrich, *The Boundaryless Organization: Breaking the Chains of Organization Structure* (Jossey-Bass, 1996).
12 Both Microsoft and Lotus introduced knowledge-management software in 2001: SharePoint and the Lotus Knowledge Discovery System. The Lotus system works on the premise that there are "digital breadcrumbs" left throughout an organization: the documents that workers create and read over the company network, and even the websites they visit. The Lotus product analyzes these materials and generates a topical index of the knowledge stored on the company's computers. It also identifies those who have created or made use of the data. This information is converted into an index of expertise, which can be accessed, shared, and exchanged among work teams across the organization.
13 Thomas A. Davenport and Lawrence Prusak, *Working Knowledge: How Organizations Manage What They Know* (Harvard Business School Press, 1998).
14 Quoted in Ikujiro Nonaka and Hirotaka Takeuchi, *The Knowledge-Creating Company* (New York: Oxford University Press, 1995), p. 7.
15 Brendan Intindola, "GE seen thriving on Welch ethos after he retires," Reuters, September 21, 2000.

16 Dave Ulrich, Norm Smallwood, and Jack Zenger, "Building your leadership brand," *Leader to Leader*, Winter 2000.
17 Charan and Colvin, "Why CEO's Fail".
18 Slater, *Jack Welch and the GE Way*.
19 Ray Stata, "Organizational learning – the key to management innovation," *Sloan Management Review*, Spring 1989.

3 Chart the Company Course

Unless we change our direction, we are likely to end up where we are headed.

— old Chinese proverb

Purpose of This Chapter

This chapter describes the challenge of communicating the direction in which the company is headed. We introduce a process that starts with purpose, mission, and vision clarification — mechanisms that provide direction and inspiration to the members of the organization. Tools that provide guidance and boundaries follow them. Next, we introduce at a high level the cogs that translate strategy to action: capabilities, processes, and projects. We conclude with an overview of a low-overhead, highly iterative planning process that keeps the gears well oiled and aligned so that the organization can adapt as business conditions change.

Often company leaders are referred to as the captains of their ships. Even leaders of small companies find themselves in charge of a "fleet" operating on global seas. Although in complete control of the ship and crew, captains are at the mercy of the elements, with only some degree of predictability. Despite environmental uncertainty, frequent obstacles must be avoided and occasional opportunities must be acted upon. The corporate ship must progress — leaving a trail of performance commitments made and met.

Capable Companies have the ability to chart a productive course to business value and the ability to navigate around that course with great agility through a series of course corrections and business transformations.

The Challenges

Given the surety that most of the assumptions that lead to a company's business strategy will change, business leaders are challenged to build a company that is both stable and adaptable. Effective company navigation demands:

- Setting the course – ensuring that employees, customers, suppliers, and investors have a shared mindset of where the company wants to be in the long run and where it is headed for the moment.
- Reading local charts – setting a course with a multiple of "goal states" to accommodate local needs demanded by global operations.
- An agenda for action – designing operating plans for potential future business environments and goal sets.
- Scenario planning – assessing which of the situations are in play at the time.
- Picking the right course – the one that minimizes risk and maximizes value.
- Making mid-course corrections – the ability to jump from one course to another while maintaining some headway toward a set of goals.

Setting the Course

Companies prepare themselves for ongoing competitiveness in many ways, but there are just a few high-leverage tools that they can employ to communicate strategic intent:

- A statement of *Purpose* describing why the company exists.
- A statement of *Mission* describing what the company strives to do, for whom, where, and to what extent.
- A statement of *Vision* describing a view of the company as it will be seen in the future by its customers, employees, suppliers, and investors.
- A statement of *Core Values* delineating what is fundamentally important about how the company and its employees behave as they venture toward the future vision.
- A statement of *Strategy(ies)* describing how the company will win in its industry, utilizing its finite resources to differentiate itself positively from its competitors, maximizing its relative strengths against the forces at work in the business environment to satisfy customer needs.

We see these five communication tools applied in many ways. Sometimes they are quite explicit and other times only communicated through corporate folklore. Often, only a few of the elements are employed. Shared understanding of and commitment to current course, speed, and goals are quite clear in Capable Companies.

Figure 3.1 Communication Tools for Clarifying Strategic Intent

There is a hierarchical relationship among these elements, building in detail and becoming more volatile from Purpose to Strategy (see figure 3.1).

The remainder of this chapter examines each of these tools in detail.

Direction and Inspiration

In their book *Jumping the Curve: Innovation and Strategic Choice in an Age of Transition*, authors Nicholas Imparato and Oren Harari state:

> Thirty years ago Peter Drucker advised executives to ask the question: What business are we in? Today we can up the ante by challenging leaders and organizations to choose what they stand for. To say that an organization "stands for" profits says nothing at all. Yes, every organization needs profits just like every body needs food...but it is as absurd to say that the Purpose of an organization is to make money as it is to say that the Purpose of a human being is to eat or breathe.[1]

Many companies fail to isolate Purpose as a singular statement, or believe that it is inferred within the Mission statement. Sometimes the company Purpose may be inferred from a company motto or from the words of a founder or Chief Executive. Sometimes they are written. Often they are not. Failure to explicitly isolate a Purpose weakens the communication of a company's essence and works against employee empowerment. What is important is that there is shared understanding of these concepts across the company.

A higher purpose

In contrast, outdoor-gear manufacturer Patagonia has existed from the get-go to use business to inspire and implement solutions to environmental preservation issues. Patagonia is clearly in the outdoor wear business. However, this business has a clearly stated Purpose that extends way beyond the obvious. Outdoor clothing represents a strategic activity used to fulfill its Purpose. The following quotation comes from Patagonia's website:

> Ours is an introspective company. When you exist for something bigger than the bottom line, you need clear vision, values and guiding principles. Ever since we first urged climbers to go easy on the rock, we've been sensitive to our role in the world as a company.

Data-storage company StorageTek's Purpose is short and sweet:

> To expand the world's access to information and knowledge.

A statement of Purpose that truly and concisely establishes the highest level of guidance for why the company will engage in business sets broad or narrow boundaries on its Mission and subsequent drivers of action throughout the company.

Mission

The Mission statement narrows the scope of possible ways that the company will engage in business by describing product types, customer types, geography, etc. Mission statements provide focus, but they do not state how the goals of the company will be accomplished.

The following are some Mission statements that reflect this level of abstraction:

- The Salvation Army: To preach the gospel of Jesus Christ and to meet human needs in His name without discrimination.
- Deluxe Checks: To provide all banks, S&Ls, and investment firms with error-free financial instruments delivered in a timely fashion. Error-free means absolutely no errors; timely means a 48-hour turnaround.
- Otis Elevator: To provide any customer with a means of moving people and things up, down, and sideways over short distances with a higher reliability than any similar enterprise in the world.

Management should be able to look to the Mission statement first to assess the appropriateness of possible courses of action. These actions must be assessed for compatibility with the Mission. For a business that is clearly established as a retailer, starting a consumer-financing division is apparently far afield from the retail business, but the company's Mission would heavily influence the appropriateness of such a move. If their Mission was tightly focused on retail (i.e., resale of consumer products), then such a move would likely be inappropriate. But if their Mission is to meet the needs of a certain consumer segment (i.e., provide consumer goods to middle-income Americans), then the action is not necessarily inconsistent. A statement of Purpose is a backstop should the Mission statement fail to cover the issue.

When the most advantageous course for a company violates its Mission or Purpose, both must be changed and communicated widely to avoid breaking down the guidance hierarchy that they establish. Similarly, such changes will likely involve recommitment by employees, shareholders, and customers to the company and its ideals. Such commitment comes from personal alignment with the company's Vision for the future.

Vision

A Vision statement is the most powerful motivator at leaderships' disposal. Vision describes "where and when" – it paints a compelling picture of the company at some future point in time. President John F. Kennedy's challenge to land a man on the moon and bring him back safely before the end of the decade is a classic example of a Vision. In his statement there was no question as to where the United States was going and what constituted success. With this Vision firmly implanted, the focus and energy of all parties involved immediately moved to strategizing "how to make it happen." Vision statements can be short, such as Microsoft Corporation's "A PC on every desktop and in every home," or lengthy, as in the case of Intuit, Inc.'s "Vision for 2010" found on their website:

> Intuit is the preeminent provider of automated financial solutions for small businesses and individuals. We are renowned as the company whose leadership and revolutionary innovations in financial services and software have delivered breakthrough value to our customers in every facet of their financial lives: banking, borrowing, investing, and beyond.
>
> We are a large, growing, multinational company. Both our competitors and our shareholders respect us for our continued ability to create and establish leadership in huge, new markets.
>
> Intuit's customer focus is legendary. Our unwavering devotion to outstanding quality – in our customer care, as well as in our products and services – inspires our customers' confidence and enthusiasm.

> Our products and services strike a careful balance between evolution –
> seeking out, understanding, and responding to our customers' needs and desires
> – and revolution – continually delighting our customers with valuable new ideas
> they haven't even thought of.
>
> People around the world use our products and access our services both on the
> PC and other computing devices. We have become an integral part of their daily
> lives. Our customers rely on our solutions to help them simplify and organize
> their finances, make better financial decisions, save money, and do it all quickly,
> easily and with greater confidence thanks to our tools, information, and services.
>
> Even though Intuit is known for the quality of its products and services, we
> know that the quality of our people is the foundation of our success.

The statement is remarkably bold in that it discusses the businesses and industries that they will be in, their position within them and their reputation. It describes the legacy that they've created (at this future point in time) from servicing customers with a focus on quality; the balance between "evolution and revolution" that drives the products that they've created; and the fact that these products have become an integral part of the daily lives of their customers.

While leaving plenty of room for the influence of unknown variables, they have painted a detailed and compelling picture of a destination point in the future. Leaders can truly evaluate the plans and strategies they are developing to assess whether they get the company closer to realizing their Vision.

Vision propels a company forward, even in the face of discouraging odds. If it is compelling and meaningful, individuals will embrace it on a personal level and go to great lengths to make it happen. Every employee of a company should be able to talk to it and about it, and explain how their daily activities contribute to its realization. If they cannot, then the Vision probably hasn't been developed at the right level of abstraction, or management has not developed a compelling case.

The level of abstraction of Vision statements allows them to persist over time, even in business environments where the power, vigor, and competitiveness forces are immense. For example, during a 1999 speech announcing the Windows CE operating system for portable devices, Microsoft Chairman Bill Gates announced that Microsoft would be revising its original Vision of "a computer on every desk running Microsoft software," inferring that this context was limiting in a world that was seeing the explosive growth of portable devices. A new Vision arose of "anytime, anyplace, any device – leveraging our software and PC assets." "This is the first time in our 25-year history we've actually changed our Vision statement," said Gates.

Twenty-five years of consistency is a great example of persistent Vision. It is a credit to Bill Gates that he recognizes the need to explicitly change it so that Microsoft employees will be empowered to explore opportunities in new areas that previously would have appeared to be inconsistent with the stated direction of the company, and so that customers, suppliers, and other stakeholders will be aware of new forces in the marketplace.

Implications

Purpose, Mission, and Vision are the cornerstones that guide strategy creation and action. Despite their importance, there is a wide disparity among individuals' definition of them and their resultant response to each. Similar confusion exists with respect to their hierarchical interdependence. Confused definitions coupled with ambiguous or non-existent statements create an environment that fosters dysfunctional, counterproductive, and unaligned or misaligned behavior.

In an article, "Built to Flip," published in *Fast Company Magazine, Built to Last* author Jim Collins captures such misalignment with the following observation:

> We can all point to companies that should have viewed themselves as "Built not to last." Confronting that reality would have helped them understand that they were never more than a project, a product, or a technology. Lotus, VisiCorp, Netscape, Syntex, Coleco – all of these companies would have served themselves and the world better if they had accepted their limited Purpose from the outset. Ultimately, they squandered time and resources that might have been applied more efficiently elsewhere.[2]

Collins's reference to "squandered time and resources that might have been applied more efficiently elsewhere" is a classic representation of what we recognize as organization misalignment; where energy and resources expended are not synergistic and not contributing fully to the goals of the company. It is extremely important for a company to have a crystal-clear understanding of what it is about and where it is going. In most companies this is assumed to be addressed by the Mission/Vision, but factors contributing to ineffective Mission and Vision are many, including:

- Lack of a consistent basis of definition for the creation of and execution from Purpose, Mission, and Vision.
- Failure to establish hierarchical interdependence among these cornerstone elements.
- Failure to do the truly hard work of defining Purpose, Mission, and Vision to offer guidance and inspiration.
- Intentionally or unintentionally, stating Purpose, Mission, and Vision in a manner where what is stated does not reflect true intent.

Table 3.1   Summary of Purpose, Mission, and Vision

Pyramid Level	Definition
Purpose	• *Why* does the company exist? • Does it stand for something (beyond profits)?
Mission	• In general terms it describes *what* business(es) the company is in. • It describes what the company will do, what benefits it will deliver, to whom, and to what extent. • It provides a critical success premise that leaders can understand, commit to, and dramatize to others.[3]
Vision	• It paints a compelling and inspirational picture of *where* the company will be (an ideal state) at some future date (*when*), intimating how the company will look, feel, and be.

Purpose, Mission, and Vision lie at the pinnacle of the Organizational Context Pyramid (figure 3.1). They are intended to establish a "true north" for the company as well as provide inspiration for its employees. They are relatively stable and change infrequently. They may remain intact, relevant, and consistent for years.

Guidance and Boundaries

With business context and direction firmly established through the definition of Purpose, Mission, and Vision, leadership focus turns to achieving desired outcomes. Without constraints, there are infinite possibilities. But in reality, constraints exist. They can be voluntary, as defined by values, or forced by limited resources. Values and Strategy offer important guidance for determining the path stated in terms of capabilities that the company should pursue at the present time, based upon its knowledge about itself and its environment.

Core Values

Values guide choices. They describe many of the qualitative aspects of life within the organization on a day-to-day basis, and they frequently describe what is truly important to the company. Values can be written or unwritten, but *everyone knows they exist*. Virtually all aspects of a company's culture are inextricably linked to its collective and individual value system(s). Articulating Values provides everyone with guiding lights, ways of choosing among competing priorities, and guidelines about how people will work together. In other words, Values provide guidance for cohesive and uniform decision making.

Shared Values are of particular importance at the executive leadership level, not only because employees look to their behaviors for clues as to whether stated Values are still valid but also because values cannot be acted upon directly. Executive leadership controls the systems and structures such as competency models and reward systems that must change if there is going to be a shift in Corporate Values. If the systems and structures do not shift, there will be no shift in values and corresponding behaviors.

Johnson & Johnson wears its values on its sleeve and lives within the boundaries provided by it. This statement is so valuable to the company that it is translated (context and intent) into local languages to assure common understanding. Called "Our Credo," this brief statement of Values has served the company well.

We believe our first responsibility is to the doctors, nurses and patients, to mothers and fathers and all others who use our products and services.

In meeting their needs everything we do must be of high quality.

We must constantly strive to reduce our costs in order to maintain reasonable prices. Customers' orders must be serviced promptly and accurately.

Our suppliers and distributors must have an opportunity to make a fair profit.

We are responsible to our employees, the men and women who work with us throughout the world. Everyone must be considered as an individual.

We must respect their dignity and recognize their merit. They must have a sense of security in their jobs. Compensation must be fair and adequate, and working conditions clean, orderly and safe. We must be mindful of ways to help our employees fulfill their family responsibilities.

Employees must feel free to make suggestions and complaints. There must be equal opportunity for employment, development and advancement for those qualified. We must provide competent management, and their actions must be just and ethical.

We are responsible to the communities in which we live and work and to the world community as well. We must be good citizens – support good works and charities and bear our fair share of taxes. We must encourage civic improvements and better health and education. We must maintain in good order the property we are privileged to use, protecting the environment and natural resources.

Our final responsibility is to our stockholders. Business must make a sound profit.

We must experiment with new ideas. Research must be carried on, innovative programs developed and mistakes paid for. New equipment must be purchased, new facilities provided and new products launched. Reserves must be created to provide for adverse times. When we operate according to these principles, the stockholders should realize a fair return.

Johnson & Johnson officials make the best case for a relevant and vital statement of Values:

> The Corporation has drawn heavily on the strength of the Credo for guidance through the years, and at no time was this more evident than during the TYLENOL® crises of 1982 and 1986, when the company's product was adulterated with cyanide and used as a murder weapon. With Johnson & Johnson's good name and reputation at stake, company managers and employees made countless decisions that were inspired by the philosophy embodied in the Credo. The company's reputation was preserved and the TYLENOL® acetaminophen business was regained.

In their book *Results-Based Leadership*, Ulrich, Zenger, and Smallwood cite a link between Values and results:

> Leaders who understand their company's and their personal values build lasting results. In the Tylenol-tampering incident, Johnson & Johnson executives were willing to absorb short-term reduced investor results because of their overriding commitment to producing ethical drugs. Lacking clear values, rudderless leaders shift from goal to goal. With values, while actions may change, the overall direction and focus stay clear.[4]

Given the contextual framework provided by Purpose, Mission, Vision, and Core Values, Strategy options and the Capabilities to execute them are focused and bounded.

Strategic clarity

In our work with many Fortune 1000 companies, we have found the word "strategy" a much abused term. It is no wonder that companies have difficulty getting alignment around Strategy when they don't define it clearly enough for it to be executed. Here is a short-list of strategic questions many companies do not ask:

- What relationships are desired among the businesses in my company?
- How does my business create advantage?
- What is our dominant business focus?
- What is our dominant customer-value proposition?
- What work is necessary to stay in business and what work creates advantage for customers?
- What are the critical capabilities needed to execute the business strategy?

These issues are so important that we have dedicated chapter 4 to them.

Table 3.2 Summary of Core Values and Strategy

Pyramid Level	Definition
Core Values	• A set of deeply held beliefs that unify and inspire employees. • How employees see themselves and their employers. • The ideals, customs, institutions, etc., of a society toward which the people of the group have an affective regard. • They establish behavioral norms for the company.
Strategy	• How a business will win in its industry, utilizing its finite resources to differentiate itself positively from its competitors, maximizing its relative strengths against the forces at work in the business environment to satisfy customer needs and move forward toward Vision realization.

Reading the Local Charts

While restructuring a Europe-based consumer electronics company's operations, issues of localization arose frequently, bogging down strategic discussions about distribution control, pricing, and contract negotiation. After a few days the sheets on the wall had recorded over 100 issues. On average there were five variants per issue. Preparing to resolve the issues, the team categorized them into several large "buckets," by the principal cause.

One group was driven by the existence of a legal entity in the country, others by language, European Community participation, etc. It was clear to the team that these localization issues were based not on the strategy that was being developed but rather by preconceptions about how any company must operate in a given country. The existence of establishing a legal entity in every company became a strategy choice, resulting in a decision to establish legal entities only where absolutely necessary and to run the others on a commissionaire basis. This decision had profound impacts on the company as a whole, making many aspects much more simple.

Some companies choose to operate as an integrated set of businesses where, to the greatest extent possible, their products and business practices are localized with the goal of appearing to be a domestic operation. Others choose to leverage their brand and their national roots by maintaining the same product and operation appearances wherever they exist. Gil Amelio, while at Apple Computer, expressed his company's product strategy as "Stand out and fit in," an expression that the team adopted, along with "Complexity is the enemy."

Companies that choose to operate in the global marketplace must have both globalization and localization strategies. Business Strategies are free of boundaries and localization. They apply to all operations with exceptions. Exceptions are driven by strategic choices as well. Once those choices are made, operation is turned over to people who know how to execute locally, just as when large ships come into port, they are turned over to pilots who know the waters and local navigation rules.

Failure to set both globalization (where, when, and to what extent we will operate) and localization (how we will operate at all locations) strategies creates opportunity for unnecessary complexity. Failure to turn over a clear strategy to a local team for execution results in false starts. When both strategies are stated in terms of Business and Organization Capabilities with performance measures, local teams can readily be empowered to create and derive value from those capabilities.

An Agenda for Action

Many companies fail to bring strategy to action because they do not translate strategy into focused and timely projects. A review of most companies' project agendas can be as confusing as reading hieroglyphics.

One can think of Capabilities as the Rosetta Stone; providing the key to deciphering the company story. However, Capabilities alone do not produce value. A company may be capable of something but not do it. Capabilities in action are business processes that deliver value. Understanding Capabilities, however, allows one to make a connection to projects that build or improve processes (see figure 3.2).

These concepts are covered in detail in chapter 4.

Table 3.3 Summary of Capabilities, Processes, and Activities

Pyramid Level	Definition
Capabilities	• What the company needs to do with varying degrees of excellence in order to execute its Strategy.
Processes and Projects	• Processes are the way that the enterprise conducts business. • Projects are the way that processes are created, improved and removed.
Activities	• The day-to-day activities that drive processes to deliver business value and drive projects to change the way that the company conducts business.

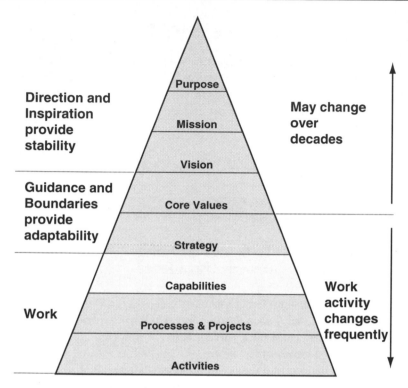

Figure 3.2 Capabilities as the Rosetta Stone

Opportunities, Obstacles, and an Ever-Changing Environment

The course to realizing Vision will be checkered with an unpredictable number of internal and external influences, causing minor and major course corrections.

We make an important distinction between Change Force and Change Driver. Whereas hundreds of Change Forces may be hitting a company at a point in time, only a few must be acted upon. For example, when Duracell entered the high-tech, high-price battery game, competitors chose to ignore this Change Force and focus on the low price end of the spectrum.

Change Forces, then, are those external and internal forces that are impacting the enterprise and may require it to move. A *Change Driver* is an individual compelling Change Force or a grouping of Change Forces that will act as a lever upon the company and force it to alter the way it does business.

Change Drivers signal the need for a specific response in the form of business capabilities.

Consider the case of companies in the data-storage business:

Industry Change Forces

1   The marketplace shifting to synergistic solutions/services.
2   The global market for storage devices will be excellent in the future.
3   The disk and networking business are growth engines and will grow exponentially due to the Internet and global needs for data storage.

Competitive Change Forces

4   New alliances and consortiums.
5   New entrants into the market, especially at the low end.

Customer Change Forces

6   Decision horizons are being shortened.
7   The average Chief Information Officer (CIO) will experience a doubling of data-storage needs every three years.
8   Increasing customer expectations.
9   Flattening budgets and tighter resource allocation.
10 Greater need and concern for power usage and impact on the environment.

Technology Change Forces

11 Increasing bandwidth (fiber) speed (MIPS) density (bytes).
12 Increasing number and type of connection and content.
13 Increasing standardization and compatibility.

> **These influences will affect every business to one degree or another and at one time or another. It is the ability to recognize the influence and to adapt or transform that distinguishes a Capable Company. Translation of strategy to a set of capabilities provides a company with a valuable pivot point around which strategic and operational planning can take place.**

One company responded in the way shown in table 3.4.

By creating a set of scenarios for each element of strategy, the set of Capabilities can be designed with a high degree of precision and can be continually assessed and aligned with "current reality."

Table 3.4 Response to Change Driver

Change Force (nos. refer to list in text)	Change Driver	Capability
2, 6, 7, 8, 11	Must increase rate of product development and delivery	• Gather and prioritize customer requirements • Design with industry standards
1, 11	Shift product focus from dedicated mass storage to networked mass storage	• Design server-specific controllers that interface with standard fibre-optic network interconnect • Design with industry standards
1, 6, 7	Customers demanding mass storage solutions that can be scaled readily and deployed rapidly	• Deliver network-attached mass storage with 30 days of receipt of order • Design network-attached mass storage for low cost of entry and 6X capacity expansion

Scenario Planning

Another workout regimen adopted by Capable Company leaders is Scenario Planning – a method that looks at multiple outcomes and sets and the likelihood of each.

Consider a manufacturing company located in the Northeastern United States that distributes 25 percent of its product across the Atlantic and 35 percent to the west of the Rocky Mountains, with 30 percent of its sales taking place between Thanksgiving and New Year's. During a particularly fierce winter, a significant number of deliveries to the west coast did not arrive in time for a critical pre-Christmas sales event, causing a third-quarter shortfall.

The failure initiated a review of the company's centralized manufacturing and product-delivery capabilities. Centralized manufacturing maximized asset utilization and process agility, but having a plant west of the Rockies minimized transportation costs and delivery risk. Meanwhile, assessment of delivery capabilities revealed that the delivery failure was more appropriately attributed to rigid delivery routes and schedules than to the location of the plant. Strategy and Capability assessment resulted in plans to locate a plant west of the Rockies in the long run and to radically increase the agility of the delivery system.

Two years later, an El Niño event washed out roads and bridges across the east–west and north–south routes to the company's customers. Fortunately, the weather-tracking, truck-location, and continual two-way communications systems that had been installed in response to the previous event enabled rapid recovery and maintenance of 99 percent on-time delivery to customers, whereas many companies' product shipments were brought to a standstill.

Scenario planning tests the strategy. Each element of the company's strategy is bracketed by a set of alternates driven by alternate scenarios for the forces that are anticipated to be in play in the future. This method reveals strengths and weaknesses for each strategy element.

Picking the Right Course

Each leg of a sailboat race is best served by a different set of sails, but wind conditions for each leg are not predictable. When a sailor prepares for a race, multiple sets of sails are laid into the hold in preparation for known and likely race conditions. Captains and navigators consider multiple scenarios, prepare for them to varying degrees, and execute an ever-changing plan to win.

Examination of multiple business scenarios should lead to design of capabilities that meet anticipated needs and can be adapted to conditions that might arise. It is useful to think of strategy and capabilities as sets of options, each of which addresses a scenario that has a likelihood of occurrence and magnitude of impact.

In our example above, the manufacturer considered two scenarios:

- Scenario 1 – There would be another transportation-limiting event (a 70 percent probability that the company would lose $140 million over three years).
- Scenario 2 – Such an event would not occur (a 30 percent probability of losing $0 over three years).

The extreme likelihood of financial and goodwill losses suggested an examination of options for transportation, plants, and warehouses. Establishing a warehouse west of the Rockies was the best financial choice, while establishing a west-coast plant was the most adaptable choice.

Construction of a new plant and changes to logistics systems resulted in a stronger company, albeit at a somewhat higher operating cost than its closest acceptable alternative.

The right complement of capabilities is the one that produces the desired return on investment at the lowest risk. Applying the logic used by financial investors to consider return, timing, and risk, thoughtful leaders build capabilities that have satisfactory return and present a high likelihood of being valuable at deployment. Their focus is on risk and timing of options that meet a return on investment (ROI) threshold, not on maximizing ROI.

A media and entertainment company faced two likely business scenarios and a profound need to replace its human resources and financial management information systems.

- Scenario 1 – Wall Street analysts could change their attitude toward multimedia companies (newspaper, radio, and TV, for example) and value them based on their integrated potential and the company would continue to operate as is; or
- Scenario 2 – The analysts would continue to value the company as the average of the valuations of each component within its sector and the company would spin off its TV assets to isolate the low multiple component.

The company is faced with a fundamental decision. Does it operate as a holding company with isolated divisions, or as an allied company leveraging resources and assets across multiple business units?

The likelihood of Scenario 1 was deemed low and its costs were high. The likelihood of Scenario 2 was deemed high and the cost of conversion to a holding company was considered to be relatively low. This led to a fundamental Corporate Strategy shift.

Given this choice, what is the capability choice around information systems? Consider two options:

- Option 1 – Implement an integrated system with "firewalls" between companies to leverage IT assets and enable a consolidated view of the holding company.
- Option 2 – Implement the same information system three times, once in each of the three companies.

An assessment of business requirements and solution attributes indicated that:

- Capability 1 – modification and maintenance of a single, integrated package would provide only adequate support for the two strategic business units; it carried high project risk and it would be costly.
- Capability 2 – two different configurations of that same package implemented once in each company presented less implementation risk and provided significantly improved business fit.

As in this case, examination of options leads to the choice of one solution from many. In other cases, analysis of scenarios along with their impacts on capabilities and associated risk will lead to choices of when to implement capabilities. Think of capabilities as a stream of possibilities, each with attendant value and risk at a particular point in time, and each becoming "ready" for deployment when its value will be maximized, its return reaches threshold, and its risk becomes acceptable.

Needless to say, capabilities that take a long time to deploy, such as enterprise resource-planning systems, office buildings, oil wells, and pharmaceutical production capacity are the most difficult to deal with. All too often, those capabilities are delivered exactly as planned but for a company that no longer exists when they become ready for use.

In addition to guiding action, scenario creation and option consideration provide superior ways of stimulating collaboration across a company. When leaders engage to build and come to a shared understanding of business scenarios, with supporting strategies and capabilities, they have a structured forum for expressing differences and synergies. The forum allows them to converge on a set of actions and to understand that those actions may be required to change if an alternative scenario becomes a new reality.

Making Mid-Course Corrections

In addition to having a pretty good understanding of what the company strives to be, every person in a Capable Company knows exactly why he or she is doing what is being done at the moment and, more importantly, has a good idea what will be done next. This is because activity in Capable Companies is focused on executing projects that enable value-adding processes or executing the value-adding processes themselves.

Companies need a breakthrough approach for rapidly realizing business capabilities to address execution issues, such as:

- Inconsistent, enterprise-wide strategy.
- Incorrect decisions made because current reality failed to take into account predictable future events.
- Constraints in the execution of their business plan caused by past business application choices.
- Key initiatives launched from functional silos, lacking alignment and fit with the greater organization with respect to process, technology, and/or organization.
- Financial planning and budgeting failing to take into account the timing and interaction between projects.

Continual Business Alignment (CBA), depicted in figure 3.3, is the term we use for this process. It is a low-overhead, highly iterative planning process that:

- Establishes a rapid-response mechanism for monitoring and responding to external and internal change forces.
- Defines the business capabilities required to achieve enterprise goals.
- Aligns business process, technology, and organizational strategies to improve operational capability.
- Defines and prioritizes critical initiatives.
- Deploys an ongoing, rapid (e.g., three-month) program/project integration cycle.

Continual Business Alignment, or CBA (described in detail in chapter 10), is a disciplined process starting with a diligent watch of internal and external Change Forces (see the traffic light in figure 3.3). The diagram reads counterclockwise from this starting point. Each matrix represents analyses and processing of inputs to specific outputs. Change Forces are analyzed and summarized as Change Drivers. Those Change Drivers then influence Business Capabilities. Capabilities are checked against Architecture Requirements

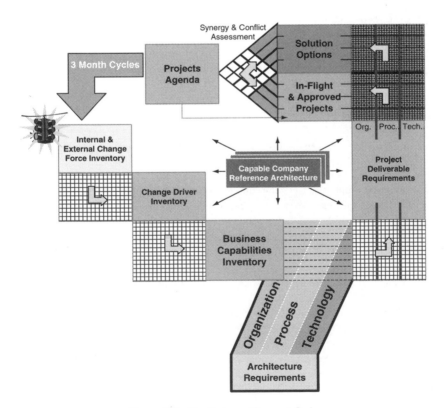

Figure 3.3 The Business Alignment Cycle

for alignment issues and additional project requirements. Projects are analyzed for integration issues, risk, and financial return. The Projects Agenda builds and adapts Business Capabilities that in turn may alter the Business Architecture – providing new alignment guidelines. To keep aligned, the Projects Agenda needs to be refreshed by repeating this cycle – we argue as frequently as once a quarter.

Assess Your Company's Adaptability

Take the quiz in table 3.5 to see if your company is ready for change.

Unfortunately, this is a pass/fail examination. Failure to answer yes to each question indicates significant risk of waste, excess complexity, inability to change, or inefficient operation.

Table 3.5 Assess Your Company's Adaptability

1	Is it clear to all leaders why the company exists?	Yes	No
2	Does each leader understand what the company strives to do in order to assure that it has a prosperous future?	Yes	No
3	It there a high degree of synergy between the reason that the company exists, what it does, and what it values?	Yes	No
4	Do leaders fully understand who their most valued customers are and what those customers recognize as value from the company?	Yes	No
5	Do all employees, shareholders, customers, and suppliers share a vision of what the company will be doing, for whom, where, and to what extent in the future?	Yes	No
6	Do most employees feel comfortable making decisions that have high customer service, supplier relationship, or financial investment risk?	Yes	No
7	Is there at least one executive accountable for the performance of every strategic business and organization capability?	Yes	No
8	Can every process executed across the company be linked to the capability that it enables?	Yes	No
9	Can every project that is being executed or planned be linked to the process that it creates or improves?	Yes	No
10	Do all leaders maintain a set of possible futures, prepare capability requirements for each, and build adaptable capability platforms to assure agility?	Yes	No

The Building Blocks of the Capable Company

- Capable Companies take a position on what they stand for and what they strive to become through clear and concise statements of Purpose and Mission.
- Capable Companies focus the delivery of business-critical information through work as well as through media. Expression of the company's Vision is paramount, followed immediately by clarity around Projects and Processes.
- Capable Companies provide their leaders with a compelling Vision of the future and establish a core set of values to guide decisions.
- Capable Companies operate day-to-day standing by their stated Purpose, Mission, and Core Values.
- Employees of Capable Companies are empowered to execute value-adding and capability-enabling processes through clear direction, trust, and desire.
- Capable Companies weigh alternative strategy scenarios and keep their options in sight.
- Capable Companies manage the tangible aspects of change through a disciplined sense-and-respond process.

Notes

1 Nicholas Imparato and Oren Harari, *Jumping the Curve, Innovation and Strategic Choice in an Age of Transition* (Jossey-Bass, 1994).
2 Jim Collins, "Built to Flip," *Fast Company*, 32, March 2000.
3 Karl Albrecht, *The Northbound Train* (New York: AMACOM, 1994), p. 20.
4 David Ulrich, Jack Zenger, and Norm Smallwood, *Results-Based Leadership* (Harvard Business School Press, 1999).

4 Make Strategy Visible

The future never just happened. It was created.

– Will and Ariel Durant

The Purpose of This Chapter

In this chapter we explore the nuances of strategic choice as they impact clarity around capabilities. No matter how well Purpose, Mission, and Vision are communicated, companies often lose direction and inadvertently steer off course. To address this clarity issue, we've created "The Capable Company Eye Chart" to test business acuity and alignment at various execution levels in the organization.

When Accenture and the Conference Board asked 500 CEOs from around the world what kept them awake at night, they found the usual suspects:

- Industry consolidation.
- Changes in type and level of competition.
- The impact of the Internet.
- Changing technology.
- Changes in supply/distribution systems.
- A shortage of key skills.[1]

Although the order of this list varied somewhat in different parts of the globe, as well as by size of company, these issues all relate to strategic response: what are the new business realities, and how are we going to respond to them?

The Challenges

It is no wonder that companies have difficulty getting alignment around strategy when they don't define it clearly enough for it to be executed. Here is a short list of questions that, when answered, help to clarify strategy for everyone in the organization:

- What relationships are desired among the businesses in my company?
- How does my business create advantage?
- What is our dominant business focus?
- What is our dominant customer value proposition?
- What work is necessary to stay in business, and what work creates advantage for customers?
- What are the critical capabilities needed to execute the business strategy?

Taking the "Capable Company Eye Chart" Test

The fears that keep leaders awake at night must be addressed in the daylight by making the strategy visible. To drive home this point, we have created a "Capable Company Eye Chart" to test the clarity of strategy in your company.

Are your strategy and its implications clear for decisive action by all levels of leaders in the company, or are things pretty blurred or difficult to see, like the chart on the right of figure 4.1?

Figure 4.1   The Capable Company Eye Chart

Like the vision eye chart, the Capable Company Eye Chart tests for:

- Myopia (nearsightedness – strategy remains fuzzy; the focus is on local agendas).
- Astigmatism (actions are not aligned to strategy).
- Farsightedness (clear about the strategy but not translated into day-to-day actions).

Note: It is probably wise to check for learning disabilities, such as corporate dyslexia, i.e., strategy being interpreted in different ways.

This chapter will provide some practical tools and prescriptions to correct strategic clarity problems in your organization.

Desired Relationships Among the Businesses

Take a look around your company. Are folks clear about the corporate strategy – do they even know what this means?

Corporate strategy defines the relationships among businesses in the corporation portfolio and the process by which investments will be determined among them.

Whether a company is *integrated* (like McDonald's), *allied* (like Xerox), or a *holding* company (like Tyco) matters in strategy execution.

Diagnosis

If you can't read the top line of an eye chart, you would be legally blind. If Corporate Strategy is fuzzy on the Capable Company Eye Chart then you are operating in the dark.

Here are a few symptoms of companies that were not clear about Corporate Strategy:

- An Allied Company acted like a Holding Company and bought 11 competency models for its different businesses. They should have bought one.
- An Integrated Company acted as a Holding Company, presented different faces to the same customer (and multiple invoices), and incurred redundant costs across sites and regions.
- An Allied Company, acting as an Integrated Company, forced the business focus and customer-value proposition of one business in another business. Competitors ate their lunch, the business unit now in turnaround.[2]

When leaders perceive a different corporate strategy, inefficiencies abound and leverage opportunities are not pursued.

Prescription

Corporate Strategy defines synergies desired among businesses in the corporation portfolio.

Be specific about your Corporate Strategy (see box) and use that choice to guide investment options and business-strategy focus.

Corporate Strategy Options:

Holding Company: wholly self-contained brands/businesses with dedicated core and support work. The businesses are tied together only by a common funding source and financial requirements (e.g., Tyco International).

Allied: each business contains the core work required to create advantage autonomously. Issues of common interest are identified and worked among businesses. Support organizations develop uniform policies and practices across geographies, tailor them to meet the needs of each business, and help achieve synergies across businesses where desired (e.g., access to customer, product files, needs to have own accounting tied to corporate). Some support work may be shared across businesses (e.g., Canon).

Integrated: single business, requiring a single business strategy for competitive advantage. Important business issues are formulated centrally and tailored for local needs to optimize the entire business (e.g. Harley Davidson or McDonald's).

For example, if a company is organized as an allied structure, then sharing technology and knowledge across borders is paramount. Take the case of Gillette, an Allied model, which shared the rubber-grip technology from its Papermate business with the grips on the new Lady Venus Razor and Oral-B toothbrushes. If a company is a Holding Company, communications across companies are of less importance than for an Integrated or Allied company.

Consider the case of an energy company that for many years operated and performed well as a regional utility. Competitive pressures and government deregulation forced the company to transform itself into an energy-service company that also provided power-generation and trading services. To separate regulated and deregulated aspects of the business, it formed a legal Holding Company with dozens of Limited Liability Companies (LLCs).

Managers of these new businesses had been successful in the past when the highly regulated industry allowed the business to be slow and plodding. Their new companies were now expected to be nimble and opportunistic. Part of the strategy called for the creation of shared IT services to leverage human capital and systems efforts. Early in the game, IT was perceived to be a roadblock, not the enabler of transformation:

- The CIO and general managers worked almost a year without being able to identify the business problems they were trying to solve.
- Three consulting teams squandered hundreds of hours trying to select a financial system; driving the President to say the project team was "trying to hit a fly with a sledgehammer."
- Database Management Systems multiplied to 11.
- General managers bypassed shared services, hired their own IT staff, and put in their own accounting systems to support their businesses.

One frustrated general manager, referring to projects on the enterprise IT agenda, said: "they really support corporate initiatives," as if they had no benefit to his LLC. The level of his frustration is directly attributable to apparent conflict between expensive enterprise investments and LLC autonomy. Lack of corporate-level concern and IT responsiveness is attributable to both the strategic transition itself and the level of shared understanding about what is important to the enterprise. The corporate CIO sees a different organization than those seen by divisional IT professionals and general managers.

Different leaders were acting under different models. Consequently, leverage and communications efforts were undermined and incorrect trade-offs were made in technology selection. Although legally a Holding Company, its desire was to act and have the capabilities of an Allied model (more like screen doors than firewalls).

Table 4.1 illustrates the implications of Corporate Strategy choice.

Since Corporate Strategy defines a number of unique businesses, it also defines the number of unique processes and enabling system requirements and the role of shared services (see table 4.2).

Getting clear about Corporate Strategy is critical but not sufficient to assure strategic success.

Ramifications of How the Business Chooses to Compete

Are leaders in your company clear about how the business creates advantage?

Table 4.1 Corporate Strategy Models

Corporate Strategy Component	Integrated (McDonald's)	Allied (HP)	Holding (Tyco International)
Business Strategy	One	Many	Many
Customers	Same	Shared	Many
Corporate Role	Resource Allocations	Define Protocols	Financial Roll-ups and Analysis
Human Capital	Common	Some shared	Independent
Systems	Common	Common	Different
Enabling Processes	Centralized	Centralized	Decentralized

Source: Adapted from Norm Smallwood, Lee Perry, and Randall Stott, *Real-Time Strategy* (Wiley, 1993).

Table 4.2 Corporate Strategy Impact on Processes

Business Impact	Process Implication
Defines the businesses in the portfolio.	Sets the general parameters for whether one or more business strategies are required and whether there is one core process for all businesses or unique cores in each business.
Establishes clear business boundaries.	Scopes the businesses that make alignment across businesses achievable.
Provides perspective about the kinds of relationships required among businesses.	Degree to which business synergies are needed.
Process by which investment choices can be determined.	Guides budgetary decisions around systems, shared services, and the like.

Business Strategy determines the way that a specific business will create distinctiveness, including the products it offers, the markets it serves, and the capabilities required to execute the strategy.

Diagnosis

If the Business Strategy is distorted, there is no clear approach to create advantage in the customers' eyes.

> **With competing business focus and customer value propositions companies wind up with project overload, competing priorities, dissatisfied customers, burn-out, and frustrated staff.**

Prescription

Be specific about your Business Strategy and use that choice to guide investment choices and get your senior team aligned around one predominant
business focus and one predominant customer value proposition.

   Business Strategy determines the way that a specific business will create
distinctiveness, including the products it offers, the markets it serves, and the
capabilities required to execute the strategy (see box). Business Strategy is
concerned with defining business focus (customer/market, product/service,
distribution, production capacity, technology) and the customer value propos-
tion (price, quality/performance, speed, service, innovation.)

> **Business Strategy**
>
> - Provides a clear business concept – we are in the business to do what with whom.
> - Defines the relationship with external customers.
> - Clarifies how business creates advantage.
> - Points to a set of core processes which define distinctiveness to the customer.
> - Identifies capabilities that need to be distinctive.

   Hamel and Prahalad provide an example of a rich strategy in their article
"Strategic Intent," where they discussed how Honda Motor Corp. pursued its
vision of becoming "the second Ford" by first establishing itself as a major
player in the US motorcycle market:

> When Honda took on leaders in the motorcycle industry...it began with
> products that were just outside the conventional definition of the leaders'
> product-market domains. As a result, it could build a base of operations in
> under-defended territory and then use that base to launch an expanded attack.
> What many competitors failed to see was Honda's strategic intent and its
> growing competence in engines and power trains. Yet even as Honda was selling
> 50cc motorcycles in the United States, it was already racing larger bikes in
> Europe – assembling the design skills and technology it would need for a
> systematic expansion across the entire spectrum of motor-related businesses.

When Honda assessed its current state and compared that to its vision state, there were tremendous gaps that needed to be bridged. Detailed assessment of gaps, threats, and opportunities revealed that the capability of designing and building cost-effective engines and drive-trains was strategic. Honda chose to develop that capability through motorcycle manufacture and then leverage it in its quest to be a major player in the automobile manufacturing business.

Business Strategy Implications on Process

A clear strategy provides criteria for making trade-offs that are critical to effective implementation and execution at process level:

- What businesses should we be in? What businesses should we not be in?
- Who are our competitors? Who are not our competitors?
- What product(s) will we offer? What products will we not offer?
- Which market(s) will we serve? Which markets will we not serve?
- What are our key capabilities? What capabilities are of less importance?
- Who are our customers? Who are not our customers?
- Which technologies will we exploit? Which technologies will we not exploit?
- Which distribution channels will we employ? Which distribution channels will we not employ?
- Which sources will we utilize? Which sources will we not utilize?

Business Focus and Customer Value Proposition

Benjamin Tregoe and John Zimmerman suggest that there are five dominant *business focuses* (i.e., the company's business strength) that determine where the business should build distinctive capability.[3]

Product/Service

- Quality of the product itself.
- Innovation around the product.
- Speed to make and deliver the product.
- Product simplification as a way to reduce cost.

Customer/Market

- Solving customers' problems; meeting customers' needs in customers' terms.
- Superior knowledge about a particular set of customers.

- Superior knowledge about this customer's customers.
- Superior customer loyalty.

Technology

- Quality of the technology.
- Market creation.
- Concept application (new customers and products for the technology).
- Innovation around the technology.

Production Capacity

- Meeting predefined product specifications.
- Qualifying requests for fit to system (keep it running).
- Improving system throughput (productivity through process improvements).

Distribution

- Accessibility through multiple distribution points.
- Sourcing of product to fit distribution channels.
- Throughput efficiencies.

There are also five possible *customer value propositions*, or ways to be recognized by customers:

Price

- It costs us less to make our products than our competitors so we can charge less. Or, we make more money than our competitors because the price for our products is fixed while our operating costs are lower.

Quality

- Our products/services are better than those of our competitors.

Speed

- We can get our products/services to our customers faster than our competitors.

Service

- We are more convenient, easier to access, and have ways of doing business that our customers prefer.

Innovation

- Our products are newer, more innovative, or more cutting-edge than those of our competitors.

Every organization should stand out from its competitors on one of these value propositions – but that doesn't mean the others are of no importance. For example, price and quality are a given in the Electronics Manufacturing Services (EMS) outsourcing market. Suppliers need to create distinctiveness – the primary reason why target customers buy a firm's products or services. Firm equity grows when customers receive the value they desire from the firm, and employees know how customer value affects their behavior.

When mapped against the company's primary Business Focus, Business Strategy is brought into focus.

Table 4.3 gives an example of several well-known companies' placement on the Business Strategy matrix.

Table 4.3 Business Strategy Matrix

Business Focus	Customer Value Proposition				
	Low Cost	Quality	Speed	Service	Innovation
Product/Service					Hallmark
Customer/		J&J			
Market					
Technology					
Production	Southwest			Northwest	Virgin
Capacity					
Distribution				Avon	

Determining your position on the matrix helps to zero in on the capabilities needed to win and the processes that deliver competitive advantage. Using company competitive data, you can also plot your competitors and determine if you are competing under the same proposition, or have a different message to your customers. For example, Delta Airlines, Northwest Airlines, and American Airlines all compete on a Production Capacity Business Focus and a Service Customer Value Proposition. Virgin competes on Innovation. Southwest competes on Low Cost.

A clear strategy provides criteria for making trade-offs explicit and diffuses office politicking.

Getting Business Strategy clear is like being corrected for nearsightedness but requiring bifocals. You still have to squint at the close-up operational details.

Identifying the Work that Creates Advantage

Note: This section is adapted from Lee Perry, Randall Stott, and Norm Smallwood, *Real-Time Strategy* (Wiley, 1993).

Work is the collection of capabilities, processes, projects, and activities.

Leaders seldom make a distinction between what work is necessary to stay in business and what work creates advantage for customers. Left to quality improvement/Six Sigma zealots, all processes should be improved. Leaders should redirect this thinking along different lines: Given the strategy, what work needs to be executed at world-class levels, and what work is OK to be at industry parity?

But are leaders in your company clear about the business processes that are critical to executing the business strategy? Can they distinguish what work is necessary to stay in business, and what work creates advantages for customers?

Diagnosis

If Types of Work is fuzzy, you're spending time and money on the wrong projects.

For example, one insurance company spent $1 million to reengineer its software change management process (someone thought that this created competitive advantage). The process was later outsourced (top management obviously thought this was necessary but distracting work that could be done more efficiently outside).

Types of Work (TOW) helps to determine competitive advantage and how to set goals.

Prescription

Being clear about the different Types of Work helps a business allocate the right level of time and resources toward building the appropriate capabilities in these areas.

Work can be classified as either *Advantage* (the work that creates distinction), *Strategic Support* (the work that enables competitive advantage), or *Business Necessity* (those activities that need to be performed at industry parity and at low cost). Collectively, these are called Types of Work (TOW; see figure 4.2).[4]

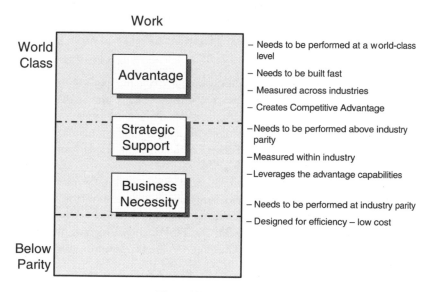

Figure 4.2   Types of Work

Relationship Among Capabilities, Process, and Work

TOW is not the same as traditional *value-added analysis*. It is a filter above it that focuses where and how value-added analysis should be applied. For example, there is value-added work in Advantage, Strategic Support, and Business Necessity work at the task or procedure level. TOW helps focus resources on creating value in advantage work and identifies where to take aim on inefficiencies or non-value-added work such as inspections and rework – especially in the Business Necessity work.

Capabilities needed to execute the strategy are realized through business processes. If a company has a *production* Business Focus and a *quality* Customer Value Proposition, the manufacturing capability is where competitive advantage is won or lost. However, within manufacturing *core process* there exists Advantage, Strategic Support, and Business Necessity work at the sub-process level (see figure 4.3).

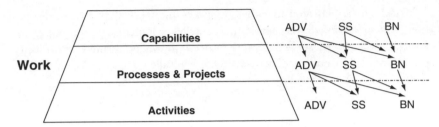

Figure 4.3   The Relationship of Capabilities to Process to Work

For example, assembly may be Advantage work but packaging may be Business Necessity and a candidate for outsourcing. Capable Companies determine which is which in order to focus investment priorities.

It is usually an eye-opening experience to have leadership teams engage in this type of conversation. Silos and other barriers usually break down as there is a filter or standard to set priorities.

TOW is also applicable to prioritization of processes (see figure 4.4).

Table 4.4 shows the results of one company's look in the mirror.

This company had difficulty prioritizing what to do and never had time to work the strategic issues. By completing the TOW exercise against their *product* Service business focus and *quality* Customer Value proposition, they realized

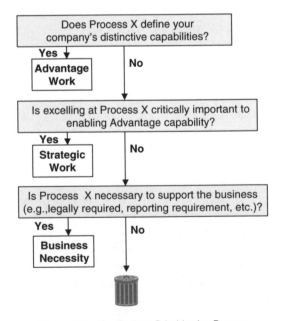

Figure 4.4   The Process Prioritization Process

Table 4.4 Types of Work Example

Business Process–Work	Advantage	Strategic Support	Business Necessity
Design			
- Key products must match proper brand image	X		
- Craftsmanship and quality image	X		
Engineering			
- Development of product specifications		X	
- Development of the part to ensure quality			X
- Integration into the vehicle		X	
- Test plan and test completion to ensure quality	X		
- Engineering release			X
- Change control			X
Manufacturing			
- Working with plants and mod centers to determine best assembly location for new projects		X	
- Determining assembly labor times/costs			X
- Developing assembly processes			X
- Launching new projects		X	
- Running mod centers			X
- Material logistics for production projects		X	
Marketing			
- Deploying integrating product into marketplace	X		
- Determining market prices by product type			X
- Developing marketing and advertising materials			X
- Developing discount structures			X
Sales			
- Creating a favorable customer experience	X		
- Development of sales web tool-configurator	X		
- Monitoring actual sales vs. forecast			X
- Identification of sales trends and why			X
- Financing in leasing process	X		
Personnel Development			
- Employee selection/hiring		X	
- Performance reviews			X
- Compensation planning			X
- Career planning			X

the critical few processes were lost in an environment where everything was equal. By focusing on the critical few processes (Advantage and Strategic Support), resources were realigned to make breakthroughs in those processes. Other work, considered Business Necessity, was targeted for cost reduction or outsourcing.

Making TOW clear makes it easier to see where the business creates the capabilities to win.

Defining Business Capabilities and Gaps

Is the organization clear about what critical *business capabilities* are needed to execute the Business Strategy?

A Business Capability is what the company needs to do to execute the strategy (e.g., support customers equally well whether via the telephone, fax, or Web). These are operational in nature. The level of performance is determined by Type of Work. The business agenda focuses on building advantage capabilities fast since competitors are trying to do the same things.

Diagnosis

If you can't make out the Business Capabilities line on the Capable Company Eye Chart, you're likely to have business astigmatism – projects are not aligned to close gaps.

We see two typical failures in strategy execution related to capabilities:

- Announce the new strategy and then try to implement it with current capabilities and traditional leadership actions.
- Announce the new strategy and at the same time describe the new leadership actions/behaviors that will be required to implement it.

Both of these approaches will fail because neither involves building the new capabilities required to implement the new strategy. Leaders have the challenge and obligation of turning strategies into future capabilities that guide leadership actions.

Taking strategy to action is not as easy as moving from current to future state with the wave of a wand.

Prescription

The only way to move from current state to future state is to develop new capabilities and align leadership actions around them.

Operationally defining business capabilities

If capabilities represent the ability and potential of an organization to execute on its strategy, they must be clearly defined.

We offer the following guidelines in developing Business Capabilities:

- Be sure that each capability is actionable.
- Make sure that each capability adequately enables an element of strategy.
- Write capability statements at an appropriate level to determine whether your company has that ability or needs to have it.
- Do not write for a specific department or function.

In drafting Business Capabilities, have subgroups work on a blank version of figure 4.5, using the following script:

1 Break the strategy down into single thoughts called "strategy elements."
2 In the hexagon shape (center), write a strategy element.
3 In the circles surrounding the strategy element, complete the statement: "to respond to this strategic element, the organization needs the ability to . . . " and write those capabilities in the next ring of circles.
4 Repeat the question about each capability and place the response into surrounding circles until the outside set of capabilities comprehensively addresses the strategy element.

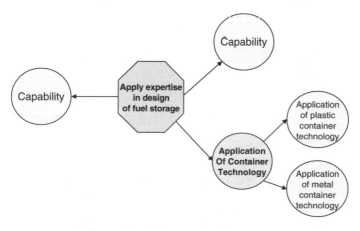

Figure 4.5 Defining Business Capabilities

Figure 4.5 gives an example for a hydrogen fuel-cell company aiming at automotive and stationary power opportunities.

At this level of detail, it is easier to determine the gap by assessing both current and desired levels (see table 4.5).

Table 4.5 Capability Gap Assessment

Existing Level	Capability	Desired Level	Gap = Desired Level − Existing Level
	Application of Container Technology		
1 2 3 4 5	Application of Metal Container Technology	1 2 3 4 5	_____
1 2 3 4 5	Application of Plastic Container Technology	1 2 3 4 5	_____
1 2 3 4 5	_____	1 2 3 4 5	_____
1 2 3 4 5	_____	1 2 3 4 5	_____

Table 4.6 Prioritizing Capabilities

Capability	Gap = Desired Level − Existing Level	Type of Work (Advantage, Strategic Support, Business Necessity)	H/M/L	Actions
Application of Metal Container Technology				
Application of Plastic Container Technology				

Key

Gap		Business Necessity	Strategic Support	Advantage
	>2.5	Medium	High	High
	1.5–2.5	Low	Medium	High
	<1.5	✕	Low	Medium

In the fuel-cell company example, the organization excelled at metal-container technology but fell short on plastic-container application capabilities. If left at the higher-level capability (container technology), they would have not identified the gap.

The next step is to determine the priorities for action by recording the gap and TOW. Using the key provided in table 4.6, record the priority and actions required.

From Capabilities to Projects

To acquire a particular capability, a business can either buy it in from outside or launch a business process *project* to create or improve that capability.

Diagnosis

Linking Projects to Capabilities and the Process that delivers them helps set the project agenda. If the Projects line on the Capable Company Eye Chart is fuzzy, benefits will be elusive.

Prescription

The Chicken or the Egg?

What comes first, Capability or Process?

In chapter 3 we said Capabilities alone do not produce value. A company may be capable of something but may not do it.

> Capabilities in action are business processes that deliver value. Understanding what work creates advantage helps focus on what capabilities are most important to execution of the strategy. The capability is executed through business process and measured by the company scorecard.

We maintain that Business Capabilities, executed through Projects, are one key to delivering the right business results. The other key is how leaders deliver the right results in the right way.

Company DNA under the Microscope

How does an organization achieve its Business Capabilities and execute Projects?

Organization Capability is defined here as how the people in an organization get things done. These capabilities cut across the organization and give the company its culture and leadership edge.

Diagnosis

If you can't read the Organization Capabilities line in the Eye Chart, there is a high likelihood that you have a virus that could cause blindness if not addressed.

Untreated, leadership teams will become dysfunctional:

- No accountability.
- Poor collaboration.
- Slow speed of change.

For example, one customer described a supplier's internal virus in this way:

> They have the slowest response time from headquarters of anyone. The lack of HQ teamwork is evident. I think they fight a lot.

As a point of clarity, we make a distinction between organization capabilities and competencies: individuals have competencies, while organizations have capabilities. Both competencies and capabilities have technical and social elements, as shown in table 4.7.

Table 4.7 Competencies vs. Capabilities

	Individual	**Organizational**
Technical	Functional competencies	Business capabilities
Social	Leadership competencies	Organization capabilities

Prescription

Define and build organization capabilities. They are the future source of sustained competitive advantage.

- Talent – Intellectual capital, know-how, competencies, commitment, workforce, employee results, career orientation.

- Speed – Agility, adaptation, flexibility.
- Learning – Knowledge management, best practices, coordination, boundaryless behavior, collaboration.
- Shared mindset – Cultural change, transformation, firm identity, firm equity, firm brand, shared agendas.
- Accountability – Performance, execution, implementation.
- Collaboration – Governance, coordination, network organization, teams to drive efficiencies, leverage.[5]

Once a company has developed organization capabilities that enhance its desired business capabilities it has achieved a sustainable competitive advantage. This cannot be quickly imitated.

Example 1
A regional utility located in Louisiana, USA. Company must continue to be successful in its base business – the regulated utility industry – while learning to thrive in new areas that are deregulated.

The leadership team has determined key Business Capabilities that are critical to its success, such as:

- Provide on-line brokering for commodity trading.
- Un-bundle and then re-bundle services.
- Incubate new services then spin them off.

We would be very surprised if at least some of the company's competitors don't have a similar list. Building the right Business Capabilities is just half of the solution. The other half is to build Organization Capabilities that enhance the business capabilities.

The company's leaders need to build the capabilities of accountability, speed of change, and collaboration for working in a deregulated industry. They also need to build the capability of learning. In the new deregulated businesses, leaders must benchmark other successful companies and bring that information into the company. They must seek out pockets of innovation that already exist around important business capability areas and then generalize these innovations to other parts of the organization. To do this they could transfer people who were in the pocket of innovation to another area; they could build information systems that help to generalize the learning; or they could utilize technology to create communities of interested people.

Example 2
Quantum Technologies is an alternative fuel company defining a new market space. Their strategy is to win share in that new space by applying expertise in design and integration of fuel-storage, metering, and electronic-control technologies to provide customers with the most effective system solutions.

Like the utility company, they have taken the time to define what will give them competitive advantage:

● Turn lab concepts into commercial products.
● Provide client solutions/systems – not components.
● Assemble core "product sets" that are readily adaptable to client needs.

Additionally, they have defined other business capabilities that are needed to operate the business efficiently:

● Develop price quotations in 24 hours.
● Generate partnership agreements.

As shown in table 4.8, the art of effective leadership is to enable Business Capabilities through the Organization Capabilities.

Table 4.8 Linking Business to Organization Capabilities

Business Capability	Organization Capability	Evidence
Turn "lab concepts" into commercial products	**Talent**	Recruit and nourish intellectual capital, know-how, and competencies
Provide client solutions/systems, not components	**Learning**	Train product developers on best practices around voices of the customer and provide opportunity to observe lead users
Generate partnership agreements	**Collaboration**	Partner with other fuel-cell players in the OEM's network

To address strategic clarity, we used "The Capable Company Eye Chart" to test business acuity and alignment at various executive levels in the organization. After applying the prescriptions recommended in this chapter, hopefully your company's strategy is clearer to those responsible for executing it.

CORPORATE STRATEGY

BUSINESS STRATEGY

TYPES OF WORK

BUSINESS CAPABILITES

PROJECTS

ORGANIZATION CAPABILITIES

The Building Blocks of the Capable Company

- Leaders in Capable Companies accept the challenge and obligation of turning future strategies into future capabilities and leadership actions.
- Capable Companies make their Corporate Strategy clear as to inter-company synergies and the role for shared services, and the trade-offs necessary in enabling support systems.
- Capable Companies go the extra step in strategic planning, articulating their business focus and value proposition so that Business Capabilities can be prioritized and a clear message is communicated to the troops.
- Capable Companies realize that not all work is created equal. They analyze their portfolio to improve on those capabilities that give them competitive advantage.
- Capable Companies align projects to capabilities and are very serious about project management.
- Capable Companies recognize that it is not enough to develop Business Capabilities. They also clearly articulate the Organization Capabilities essential for winning and build these capabilities into their culture.

Notes

1 "What CEOs Worry About," *Business 2.0*, April 17, 2001, p. 90.

2 This example comes from our observations at Gillette in 1999. In Gillette's 2001 Annual Report new CEO James Kilts admits to the harm done by forcing Gillette's blades strategy on portable power (Duracell). It cost Duracell 21 consecutive months of market-share decline and 7 share points in the US share market. After they reversed this strategic mistake, Duracell had 7 months of consecutive market-share growth. In an allied company, each business unit must determine its business focus and customer-value proposition.

3 Benjamin B. Tregoe and John W. Zimmerman, *Top Management Strategy* (Simon & Schuster, 1980).

4 Norm Smallwood, Lee Perry, and Randall Stott, *Real-Time Strategy* (Wiley, 1993).

5 For more on organization capabilities see Dave Ulrich and Norm Smallwood, *Why the Bottom Line Isn't* (Wiley, 2003).

Part II Delivering Value

The corporation as we know it, which is now 120 years old, is not likely to survive the next 25 years. Legally and financially, yes, but not structurally and economically.

– Peter Drucker

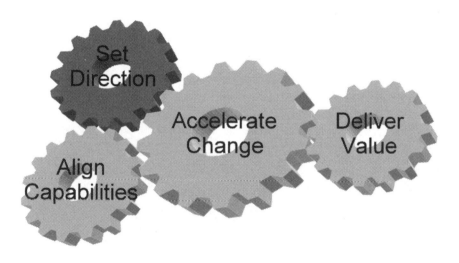

5 Build the Value Exchange

It is better to know some of the questions than all of the answers.

– James Thurber

The Purpose of This Chapter

How to create value for customers, employees, and investors is the subject of this chapter. Capable Companies execute on their value exchange by determining the right products and services, then assuring the capability to deliver them. Attention is paid to balancing infrastructure and superstructure, including creating alignment across customer and supplier boundaries to deliver value.

Leadership in most companies will espouse some form of "the customer is king" philosophy, using the external party who exchanges hard currency for the company's products as their definition of a Customer. In 1992, Karl Albrecht wrote a little book with big ideas, *The Only Thing That Matters*. Many leaders have taken the central theme of the book – "The whole organization should be one big customer service department" – out of context when they limit the scope of customer to representing only outside parties.

In fact, companies manage a chain of *Value Exchanges,* beginning with shareholders investing in the potential of a company and ending with customers investing in the company's products (goods, services, and information) and being satisfied with the value derived from them. Capable Companies understand their *Value Exchange System* and build capabilities to create and maintain long-term relationships among all constituencies.

The Challenges

Creating value for customers, employees, and investors is not as simple as it used to be. Some of the challenges companies face include:

- Determining the right products, services, and talent for the exchange model.
- Articulating the Value Exchange in a way that customers readily endorse.
- Making the right choices on acquiring capacities.
- Building the requisite capacities and partnerships.
- Balancing the infrastructure and superstructure.
- Creating alignment in a boundaryless world.

Determining the Right Products and Services

Frequently a company's Value Exchange System is quite simple. For example:

> We choose to be in the retail fuel-oil business. We buy fuel oil from wholesalers, we store it for as little time as possible, then we deliver it to homeowners. Our product is fuel oil. Our customers are homeowners. We excel at keeping our homeowners' fuel tanks more than one-quarter full at all times.

This company is quite focused and its simplicity provides an insight into how companies, both large and small, benefit from having a clear view of their Value Exchange System. In this case, the system works as shown in figure 5.1.

Strategically, this company has chosen a Product Business Focus with a Service Customer Value Proposition. That is to say that a single product (fuel oil) will be sold to as many customers (homeowners) as possible, and the company will differentiate itself from its competitors through Service, delivered in the form of the assurance that "there will always be fuel oil in your tank." As simple as this may be, many companies fail to recognize and/ or explicitly state their Business Strategy and, as a result, find valuable resources being wasted on non-strategic pursuits.

Our simple fuel-oil company is clearly an integrated enterprise, indicating that regardless of how many locations it might have, it should work hard to avoid duplicating any of its strategic components. To complement its Corporate

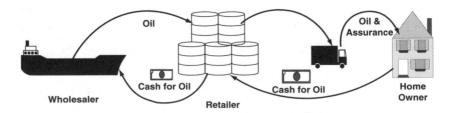

Figure 5.1 The Value Exchange System

Strategy, the company has adopted an operating tactic that is based on selling a single product and differentiating on the basis of service. This is one of several *Business Archetypes* that clarify how a company should focus its resources. Table 5.1 shows a family of Business Strategy Archetypes and implications related to those various choices.

Having established a Product/Service business focus as its Business Strategy, our fuel-oil company's growth will be derived from adding more homeowners to its customer list, although table 5.1 might suggest selling more products to existing homeowners.

This was the case for a number of natural-gas distribution companies across the United States. Energy utilities faced impending deregulation and subsequent consolidation of their industry. One such company built a set of future state scenarios, and most of them indicated a high likelihood that the company would be acquired by a larger fuel utility within three to six years. Facing that prospect, it chose to maximize value to its shareholders by increasing its market value. To do so, it evaluated its portfolio of resources that included its pipelines, storage capacity, customer base, delivery technology, and distribution capacity.

Table 5.1 Business Strategy Archetypes

	Product/ Service	Customer/ Market	Technology	Production	Distribution
Characteristics	• Tied to a product or service • Future products resemble current and past products • Products made to satisfy customers • Seek new customers	• Anchored to a class of customers • Identifying customer needs is crucial • Products made to satisfy customer needs • Destiny in the hands of customers	• Ability to apply technology capability to create or improve products or services • Solutions looking for problems • Market creation is a key capability	• Utilize capability or resource • "Keep it running" or "keep it full" • Optimize unit cost • Full capacity is the key to profit-ability	• Unique way of getting products/ services to customers • Sell anything that can be pushed through the distribution process
Examples	• Ford Truck Division • GE Aircraft Engines • Hallmark	• Johnson & Johnson • Rockwell Autonetics • Nike	• 3M • Evans & Sutherland • DuPont Kevlar	• Marriott Hotels • Delta Airlines	• PG & E • Avon • Wal-Mart

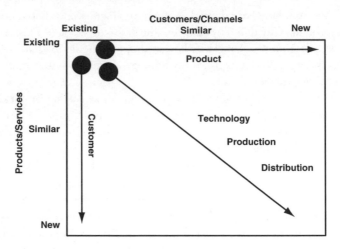

Figure 5.2   Growth Strategies

Whereas the company had invested heavily in distribution (pipe safety and supply assurance), it found that its customer base and service capabilities were its greatest and most leveragable assets, suggesting a shift from a Product/ Service Business Focus to one based on Distribution. Partnering with cable and satellite television and appliance manufacturers afforded the opportunity to leverage its customer-service center, fleet of service vehicles, and capable service personnel to deliver more products through its existing channel, initiating a growth strategy that is Distribution- rather than Product-based.

As figure 5.2 suggests, companies pursuing a Product strategy will seek growth from selling existing products to new customers. A Customer strategy company, on the other hand, looks to grow by selling new products to existing customers. Companies with a Technology, Production, or Distribution strategy look for growth opportunities in both ways.

Transitions such as these are commonplace. The clarity of what must change, alignment around the change, and the ability to transform capabilities are what makes one company more successful than the other during such transitions.

Making the Right Choices on Acquiring Capabilities

Understanding the elements of a company's Value Exchange System leads to the identification of the critical capabilities that enable business success.

Take the media and entertainment industry as an example. Who is the customer? Is it the viewer of television programs, the reader of magazine articles, the listener who tunes into the radio, or the advertiser who buys time slots or magazine space? Can companies survive and thrive while serving two masters? The Value Exchange System diagram shown in figure 5.3 illustrates how one multimedia and entertainment company makes money.

Start at any oval noun, and read the action in the rectangle that influences the connected oval. For example, "Promotion" "Drives" "Realized Audience," which in turn "Establishes" "Ratings."

A quick tour of the system clarifies the relationships that drive revenue and business success. Beginning at the lower right and working counter-clockwise:

- Magazines and television/radio stations create the capacity to distribute various types of content to audiences. This potential size of the actual audience is referred to as "reach."
- Promotion and content selection (e.g., television or radio programs, magazine articles) create smaller audiences with desirable demographic or lifestyle characteristics.
- The combination of Demographics and Ratings creates a valued Potential Audience (products) that are sold to advertisers (customers).

It is not surprising that this company behaved like two companies. Most of the company and its resources focused on content and audience, and only a few committed themselves to advertisers. After clarifying the company's value

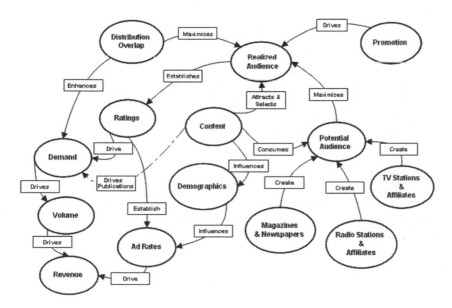

Figure 5.3 Value Exchange System Diagram

Table 5.2 How Value Is Created

Value-Adding Element	How Value Is Created
Price	It costs us less to make our product and therefore we charge our customers less for it.
Quality	Our products are better than those of our competitors.
Speed	We deliver our products more quickly than our competitors.
Service	We are easier to do business with than our competitors.
Innovation	Our products are newer, more cutting-edge, and state-of-the-art than our competitors'.

proposition, it became much easier to get everyone working to build value for customers through highly selective audiences.

Table 5.2 summarizes key points from the discussion in chapter 4.

In this case, the Value Exchange is to be built around Quality of products offered and Speed of delivery. By implication, Quality and Speed demand strategic focus while Price, Service, and Innovation must be maintained at a par with competitors.

Building Requisite Capabilities and Partnerships

"We innovate in everything that we do." Companies are tempted to make such statements to establish an image. Others include "The customer is always right" and "We will control every aspect of our destiny." These statements represent strategies that do more to limit success than to encourage it, because they create a limitless set of options for what the company must be really good at and how its employees will choose to work. The two companies described above have made hard choices regarding customers and products. Additional choices about the work required to create value can profoundly impact a company's ability to stand out in its marketplace. Such choices involve what work needs to be done, by whom, where, and to what extent.

Vertical integration, cooperative partnerships, centers of expertise, in-sourcing, and outsourcing all represent means by which companies acquire the set of capacities needed to produce value. Choices among these and other options must complement the Value Exchange Strategy and optimize the Value Exchange System. The first step in the process is to map out the business process and reveal the work that must be done.

For a technology-driven company, success (advantage) lies in its ability to maintain leadership through its invention and to continually create new ways of applying that invention. Take the case of a leading manufacturer of high-fidelity sound products for consumers. In the mid-1960s, the company patented a sound-reproduction system that added reflected sound to the direct sound that its competitors' loudspeaker systems reproduced. This combination became the basis of the company's success. In the early years, the company's competitive advantage was derived from its ability to design enclosures that afforded the loudspeaker its potential. Consequently, the company outsourced all of its loudspeaker and enclosure production and focused on engineering and assembly, to assure product quality and a continual stream of new products to employ the patented technology.

As competitors' products closed the sound-quality gap through various means, the company took its next technology step by patenting a new way of building the loudspeakers themselves. To protect its patent, the company in-sourced the manufacture of loudspeakers and started to design a new line of loudspeaker systems based on the new technology. As time progressed, the cycle of outsourcing production of a commodity item, patenting an innovative replacement technology, then in-sourcing manufacturing of the patented technology continued whenever strategic advantage changed. Each cycle caused the company to reassess its classification of capabilities as Advantage, Strategic Support, and Business Necessity capabilities.

As we outlined in chapter 4, the first step is to consider how the company wants to win, as shown in figure 5.4.

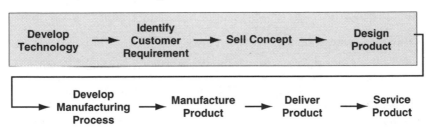

Figure 5.4 Technology-Focused Company Process Flow

Source: Norm Smallwood, Lee Perry, and Randall Stott, Real Time Strategy (Wiley, 1993).

Next, consider each business process that is executed in the course of current business operations. By applying the sorting logic described in figure 5.5, each process can be classified into one of four types. Only the top two, Advantage and Strategic Support Processes, deserve a great deal of attention. The resource demands of Business Necessity should be minimized.

This method clarifies where Innovation can add value, and which aspect of business operation the company must control. Combined with the data provided on Customer and Product-Value Creation, it also establishes where customer requirements fit into the Value Exchange System.

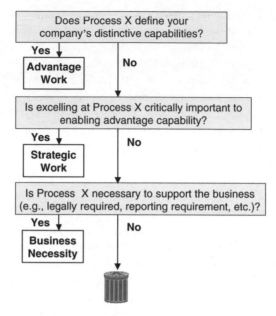

Figure 5.5   The Process Prioritization Process

Table 5.3 sorts out work that is done in the manufacture of loudspeaker systems. It demonstrates a way of maximizing leverage from internal and external resources.

Table 5.3   Sourcing Options

	Business Necessity Work	**Strategic Support Work**
Demands unique company knowledge	**Manage for Efficiency** • Coil winding at lowest cost and highest yield. • Loudspeaker-system assembly at shortest cycle-time and cost.	**Own the Process** • Assemble loudspeaker drivers and protect the process. • Manufacture plastic parts for Product X enclosure.
Does not demand unique company knowledge	**Contract Out** • Wood cabinet manufacture. • Customer service and product repair.	**Broker the Process** • Contract loudspeaker-cone manufacture to a trusted non-competing partner. • Contract engineering of remote-control units.

When companies apply these methods to the analysis of work, it becomes apparent that efficiency and focus are being bartered against control and proximity. Today's Value Exchange Systems cross divisions, companies, and continents, challenging traditional views of what makes a company.

Balancing Infrastructure and Superstructure

A precision-instrument company developed a method for precision-grinding metals. In effect, this is the core competency of the company and its principal value-generating capability. Fifty years ago, this capability enabled them to produce machine parts of superior quality. Thirty years ago it enabled them to manufacture precision measuring instruments of competitive quality, so they decreased cycle-time to maintain competitive superiority. Now, it enables them to build precision instruments and machines of superior quality and value.

A single capability has sustained this company for over 45 years of continual, albeit slow growth. When the company was small, it outsourced many of its production activities such as plating, painting, and heat-treating. As it grew, it brought most of these capabilities in house to reduce cost and cycle time. Now, as growth over the past five years has caused the company to stumble a few times, it has begun shifting its capabilities back to outside service providers who have better economies of scale, so that its leadership can focus on its core competency of precision grinding and instrument assembly.

The transition to a Distributed Enterprise model (see figure 5.6) will be traumatic, because the company has never invested in the business processes or e-business technologies that execution with multiple Value Delivery partners will demand.

On the other hand, a manufacturer of cotton cloth wanted to develop what was already a very important clothing manufacturer account into a strategic partner by integrating the supply chain between the two. Working together, the companies determined that the two were insufficient to make the kind of progress that they both wanted from a strategic relationship. The cloth

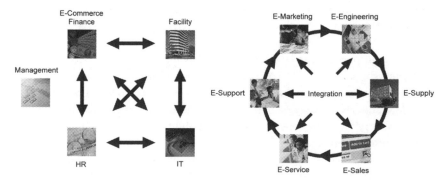

Figure 5.6   The Distributed Enterprise Model

provider needed to involve its dye manufacturer and the clothing manufacturer needed to involve at least one of its major customers.

The four companies elected to design an information-sharing portal, as shown in figure 5.7, where the end customer of the clothing manufacturer shared sales and future promotion data, the manufacturer shared stock and future finished goods data, the cloth manufacturer shared inventory and future raw materials inventory, and the dye manufacturer shared stock and future raw materials information.

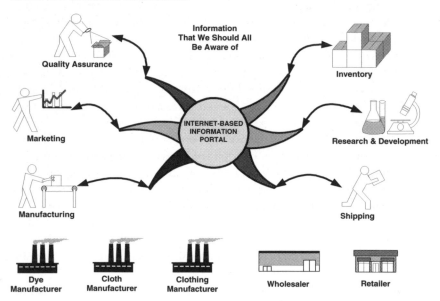

Figure 5.7   The Extended Enterprise

The revised flow of data resulted in a number of process changes, reduced inventory for all parties, shorter lead times, and ultimately lower costs. Success was based, for the most part, on each party trusting the others to do what was in the best interest of the clothing retailer in particular and the partnership in general. In effect, the superstructure of the extended enterprise leveraged the already high performance infrastructure of its members.

Partnerships where both parties take risks and share the rewards are not the only type of strategic partnerships, but they do raise the stakes above that of a simple supplier–customer exchange. The trend toward rapid business change, rapid startup, and unit-costing business capabilities favors this "virtual enterprise" business model.

Agility, discussed in detail in chapter 10, is the only competitive advantage that wins and lasts for most organizations. Agility has always been valuable, but only recently has it come to the top of the agenda. Technology has changed the rules of the business game. Every company can have worldwide reach using telecommunications and Internet technologies. Complex business capabilities such as multi-currency, twenty-four-hour, seven-days-a-week operations, and retail sales over the Internet, can be set up in a week. Even more demand for agility is derived from the transition to an experience-based marketplace. In 1970, features and functions won the deal. In 1980 it was quality. In 1990 it was service, and in 2000 it became the shopping experience.

Enough infrastructure supports the evolving superstructure of the company. Nowhere was this balancing less well demonstrated than by many of the dot. bombs and dot.coms of 1999–2000. On one end of the scale, Amazon.com built an immense infrastructure without a superstructure that could generate enough sales to pay for it. At the opposite end of the spectrum, Toys "Я" Us had more superstructure-generating sales than its technology infrastructure could support. The two companies improved their utilization of collective capacity when they joined forces to use Amazon.com's infrastructure to service Toys "Я" Us customers through the 2000–2001 selling season.

But why was Amazon.com able to create the click-driven channel when Toys "Я" Us could not? Whereas the former company could focus on building its only channel, the latter had to make a transition to a new one. The infrastructure that made it a success in the bricks-and-mortar world inhibited its success in the clicks-and-mortar world. Toys "Я" Us had a set of functional and operational boundaries that it had to break through before it could make the transition to clicks and mortar.

Alignment in a Boundaryless World

The cloth to clothing example given earlier, of four companies collaborating in mutual self-interest, describes a boundaryless environment. Alignment in such an environment is a matter of clarity of messages, mutual understanding of goals, and shared measures of success with mutual trust. With these essentials in place, each participant executes its part of the process with excellence and contributes to beneficial results for all. Delivering organizational capabilities that support Value Exchange is made much more simple when there are no boundaries constraining participation in the Value Exchange System. However, this is not to say that everyone gets involved in everything. Rather, when everyone involved knows what is expected of them, it is easier for the participants to pull together even when they are well out of sight of the leader, or in this case, the customer.

Boundarylessness expands the business environment to include customers, suppliers, investors, and even competitors. In the examples above, companies have gone to extremes to reach out and bring the customer into the center of their Value Exchange System. Each of those companies also recognizes that such transparency of operation creates a change force upon the company that must be dealt with every day. Process and product defects are visible sooner, as are the sources of defects. The ability to recognize defects and respond to them quickly is an essential capability, not an improvement option, as it has been considered in the past. Downstream customer relationships and upstream supplier relationships become more solidified, causing all parties to work harder to work together for the long haul. This forces more thought when choosing suppliers and even when choosing customers.

For all of the benefits of boundarylessness, there are an equal number of responsibilities. Companies that operate in this manner come to rely more on leadership, process, and precise value-determination. They also develop a culture where collaboration is essential and shared measures of performance encourage valued behaviors. Critical to a successful Value Exchange System is that strategic planning becomes a continual process focused on all customer constituencies and executed through continual capability alignment. The benefit of being customer-focused, value-driven, and boundaryless far out-weighs the cost of making it so.

The Building Blocks of the Capable Company

- Capable Companies view their company, its processes, and its trading partners as an integrated Value Exchange System where all parties benefit from active participation.
- Capable Companies build on their corporate strategy choice to drive business capabilities around product and customer strategy.
- Capable Companies articulate the contribution of product, customers, technology, production, and distribution and choose one as their dominant business focus.
- Capable Companies explicitly state the interrelationship among products, customers, and business processes and how they come together to create business value.
- Capable Companies understand how their products create value for their customers and they create the Capabilities to execute on that value promise.
- Capable Companies maximize agility by building only essential infrastructure and building high-performance superstructure at the same time.
- Capable Companies leverage intimate knowledge of their Value Exchange System and generate confidence in their strategies to operate throughout the extended enterprise.

6 Forge Customer Relationships

There is only one valid definition of business purpose: to create a customer.

– Peter Drucker

The Purpose of This Chapter

In this chapter, written with R. Dixon Thayer, we expand on the notion of creating and sustaining value throughout the customer experience. We begin with a quick review of the customer life cycle and then delve into capabilities important to customer-acquisition and customer-engagement models. We present ideas for rigorously mapping needs and expectations to engagement methods, mining opportunities, and providing exceptional customer service regardless of how valued customers come into contact with the company. We conclude with thoughts about retaining customers and leveraging new opportunities from them – additional fuel to keep the company moving forward.

Once a company determines its Value Exchange with customers, attention shifts to how they attract, convert, fulfill, and leverage profitable customers.

Depending on the company's value proposition, these capabilities will vary in scope and priority. For example, at Quantum Technologies (QT), the industry shift toward alternative fuel cells in the OEM market required the following new *customer relationship management* (CRM) capabilities:

- Manage customer contracts and relationships for full "Life-Cycle Profitability."
- Customize product-value proposition to the client.
- Understand customer expectations before responding to a Request for a Quote (RFQ).
- Design, market, and sell "Client Solutions" that continuously create a unique market space.

- Continuously increase the real and perceived value of the Client–QT relationship.
- Assemble core "Product Sets" that are readily adaptable to client needs, can be deployed rapidly, and can be operated cost-effectively.
- Quickly respond to new opportunity.
- Rapid response to RFQ with good cost estimates within 24 hours (not to 5 decimal accuracy) with one focal point.

The Challenges

Regardless of Value Exchange model and value proposition, most companies face the following challenges:

- Making the value proposition clear throughout the customer experience.
- Attracting the right customers.
- Converting prospects and browsers.
- Fulfilling customer needs and guaranteeing the experience.
- Organizing delivery to customers when multiple partners are involved.
- Building loyalty and retaining customers profitably, while leveraging new business.

The Customer Life Cycle

Customer satisfaction lies behind a double-locked door. Identifying critical customer contacts (both direct and indirect) is the first key. The second key is the management of the business activities required to support customers.

This chapter organizes issues and capabilities around the *Customer Life Cycle* (see figure 6.1):

Attract → Convert → Fulfill → Leverage

- *Attract*: Finding potential customers demands channel-development, brand-management, product-marketing, advertising, promotion, and data-mining capabilities.
- *Convert*: Closing prospects to sales demands needs-assessment, value-proposition, and solution-proposal capabilities.
- *Fulfill*: Completing orders demands process-technology, customization, distribution, and e-commerce capabilities.
- *Leverage*: Growing the business demands new products, product enhancements, cross-selling, training, and customer research capabilities.

Customer Acquisition   Customer Loyalty

Attract	Convert	Fulfill	Leverage
• customer segmentation • channel development • brand management • product marketing • advertising • promotion • data mining • traffic generation	• needs assessment • value proposition • solution proposal • sales-force effectiveness • e-CRM	• process technology • customization • product availability • product status • credit checks • customer service • distribution • channel management • e-commerce • e-procurement	• cross-selling • product enhancements • service enhancements • training • customer research • marketing • co-marketing • customer interaction • e-CRM

Figure 6.1   The Customer Life Cycle

According to Dixon Thayer, COO of the Ford Motor Company's Diversified Consumer Services group, retaining customers profitably and leveraging opportunity has never been more important. How a company executes these capabilities has a huge impact on the bottom line.

In Thayer's model at Ford (see figure 6.2), attention is given not only to the customer-facing processes (the X axis) but to the capability shift needed to move along the business strength continuum from survival actions to regenerating new business (the Y axis).

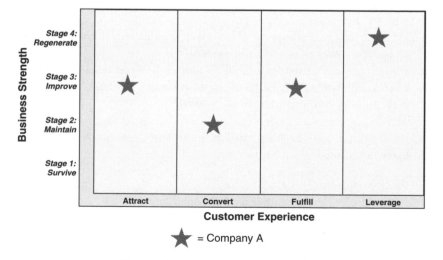

Figure 6.2   The Advantaged Business Model

The evolution a business goes through as products and services mature is what we call "business strength":

1 *Survive*: To run the business with focus on cost control through cash management, and asset maintenance.
2 *Maintain*: To hold to process standards with focus on cost reduction and efficient work management. To ensure parity in consumer-specific capabilities (i.e., speed or quality).
3 *Improve*: Continuous process improvement.
4 *Regenerate*: Create new business opportunities.

Thayer defines an "advantaged business" as one that performs in stage 3 or 4 in at least two customer experience categories. In other words, advantage occurs when a business is recognized for having a sustainable track record of generating and implementing big growth ideas while maintaining base business profitability.

Attracting the Right Customers

Take the following quiz for your company:

- Is your company recognized as a "household name" in your geographic market(s)?
- Do you think potential customers remember your company as a potential provider of services or products based on any advertising source (e.g., Web ads, TV, print)?
- Do your potential customers choose your products or services based on recognition from an advertising source?
- Is your company's knowledge of the customer (consumer research) first rate?
- Does your company make good use of customer feedback to adjust the perception of your company in the market?

If you answered "no" or "not sure" to several of these questions, you are probably not attracting the customers you want.

Customer Segmentation

The first step in developing the capabilities to attract customers is to determine your target market (see figure 6.3).

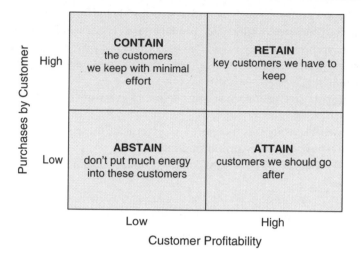

Figure 6.3   Customer Segmentation Matrix
Source: Used with permission from Results-Based Leadership, Inc.

A good example of understanding customer segmentation is the airline industry. Business fliers represent 20 percent of travelers, 70 percent of revenue, and 80 percent of profits. High attention should be paid to retaining those customers and attracting new business customers as well.

How do Capable Companies build advantage capabilities in attracting customers?

- They maintain high standards for brand and product recognition (e.g., Coca-Cola, Microsoft, IBM, GE, Nokia, Intel, Disney, Ford, McDonald's and AT&T are the world's top brands, according to *Business Week*).
- They continually develop new products for existing customers and new customers for existing products (e.g., Amazon.com).
- They create and advertise new products to their customer base before competitors can respond (e.g., Williams Energy).

Converting Prospects/Browsers into Customers

If you do attract the customers you want, how are you at converting them?

- Do enough targeted customers who have made some type of contact with your company actually purchase your products or services?

- Are you number 1 (or 2) by a wide margin in your market?
- Do your customers view your products or services as offering a unique value proposition (they would "go out of their way to" buy from you)?
- Are employees empowered and rewarded to create new ways to convert customers?
- Is prospect conversion viewed as integral to everyone's job?

If you answered "no" or "not sure" to several of these questions, you are probably letting too many prize fish off the hook.

How do Capable Companies build advantage capabilities in converting customers?

- They focus on ensuring that consumers buy products, once contacted (e.g., Nordstrom). They continually seek new and improved ways to convert existing consumers and prospects (e.g., Coke offering bottled water to increase their share of the stomach).
- They get consumers to buy something that they don't even know they need (e.g., Palm Pilot).

Much has been said and written about the importance of doing a thorough needs assessment, clarifying the value proposition to the customer in presenting a solution rather than just a product to the customer. Much of the salesforce training and automation in recent years has focused on these conversion levers. Another critical capability that is emerging is the ability of an organization to map customer needs and expectations to the engagement method.

Mapping Customer Needs and Expectations to Engagement Methods

Initiatives such as e-commerce, that are launched without a clear vision of how customers are to be engaged and what they should experience, carry significant risk of failure. Of equal importance is a clear understanding of the degree to which web-based customer interactions are integrated across the organization.

Many businesses abdicate their responsibility to harmonize their customer-engagement model, maintaining separate organizations and infrastructures based upon the way (e.g. web, retail, telephone) in which a customer chooses to interface with the company (see figure 6.4). Consequently, these businesses project the problems they refuse to address onto their customers. They do not build their organization and infrastructure from the customer inward. An IBM television commercial highlighted the problem, citing the frustrations of a woman trying to return a lamp she bought online to the bricks and mortar

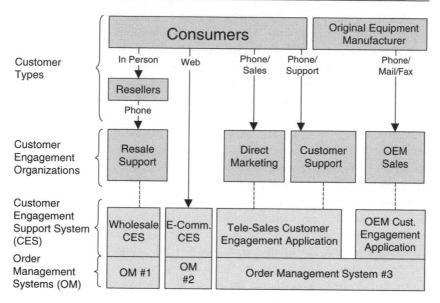

Figure 6.4 A Representative "As We Are Today" Customer Engagement Model

incarnation of the same company. The implied response from the store clerks was, in effect, "They're us, but we're not them!"

The rapid acceleration of the Internet as a direct-to-consumer (sub) channel is just the latest change force in the continuing evolution of how companies engage customers. While many companies are quick to launch technology projects to participate in the latest wave, they often fail to understand that much of the success of these efforts will depend on reconciling the business and organizational issues tied to customer engagement. Although there are certainly technical challenges, it is more a management problem.

Frequently the discussion around the Internet within a company is externally focused. This focus centers on questions such as "What are the opportunities in our industry?" or "Which Internet initiatives should we be pursuing?" What is often missing is a set of clear management decisions that establish how a customer engaging the company through this new medium will "experience the company," and how this singular experience blends with all other means of engagement such as telesales, customer support, and bricks and mortar retail.

Organizations should approach the problem from the customer's perspective to understand the issues their customer engagement model must overcome. By examining various customer types, and the ways in which they engage the company, valuable insight is gained that will drive the capability requirements that technology must support. For most companies, the IBM commercial is far too close to reality. Customers expect to engage a company seamlessly through all avenues that they present to the public.

Many enterprises, be they in the private or public sector, have approached e-commerce by generating a flurry of activity and seeing "what sticks." At least one state government entity has mandated that each of its agencies "conduct a minimum of one e-commerce initiative this year," but did not orchestrate them into a comprehensive program with aligned goals. Many others have isolated e-commerce efforts within a stand-alone division, distinctly separate from existing wholesale, bricks and mortar retail, and/or telesales business.

By not viewing e-commerce as simply an extension of existing business-to-consumer (B2C) or business-to-business (B2B) channels, companies often build a stand-alone e-commerce infrastructure. These stand-alone architectures provide static information and process basic on-line sales transactions, but are incapable of delivering the engagement experience customers expect from the business as a whole. We know of at least one company whose numerous 800-numbers connect to one of three distinct infrastructures aimed at servicing the end consumer. Based upon which number the consumer dials, the customer service representative may or may not have any knowledge of the customer's prior contacts with the company.

The customer-engagement process must be designed holistically for a business to effectively and efficiently engage customers. Companies must understand the unique types of customers that engage them and the means by which they desire to do so. They must then decide which of these avenues of engagement they will choose to support. Only then can the technical architecture and resultant infrastructure be put in place to support the capabilities that will make the desired customer engagement experience happen.

It is not uncommon for companies who explore their customer engagement processes to find serious disconnects within the infrastructure that preclude delivery of a quality customer experience. As we can see from figure 6.4, this may include:

- separate application systems that support different customer contact points (e.g. telephone vs. the Web vs. bricks and mortar);
- incompatible and/or redundant databases;
- unacceptable latency periods transferring data between systems.

Ultimately this all translates to excessive costs:

- opportunity cost in the form of dissatisfied customers who may ultimately choose to do business elsewhere;

- tangible cost associated with supporting a technical infrastructure that may well have been designed for doing business in another era.

Building consensus around a customer-engagement model is senior management's responsibility and is essential to making correct IT decisions. If such a model does not exist, IT should champion its creation before committing to an e-commerce initiative. The model should clearly highlight:

- major customer types (OEM vs. the consumer);
- the organizations and means by which the customers interact with the company;.
- the major technology platforms that support this engagement.

Often this can be accomplished with two single-page drawings, one showing the existing model, the other illustrating the desired state. (In figure 6.5, note that there is a single infrastructure for all the various ways in which the end-consumer comes into direct contact with the company.) These models can then be used to engage executive stakeholders, both individually and collectively, in dialogue that delivers consensus.

Customer engagement should be the result of explicit management decisions that clearly articulate what customer-types will be engaged through what

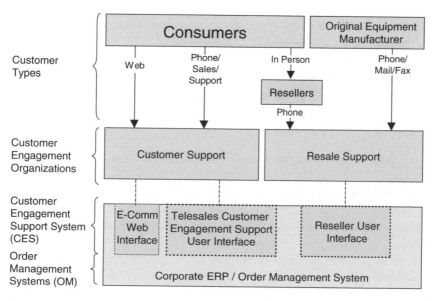

Figure 6.5 A Representative "Future State" Customer Engagement Model

means, as well as many qualitative factors that help to define the "experience" the customer has when in contact with the company, especially when the time comes to purchase.

Fulfilling Customers' Needs

Once prospects are converted to customers, how is your company fulfilling their needs?

- In describing the overall customer experience with your company, do you usually meet or exceed customers' expectations?
- Are there adequate systems in place to obtain customer feedback and adjust your processes and procedures accordingly?
- Are supply-chain partners fully integrated with your business?
- Compared to your competitors, do you have superior distribution capabilities to your current and potential customers?
- Is your customer retention/loyalty where it needs to be?

If you answered "no" or "not sure" to several of these questions, your customer may be ready to defect.

How do Capable Companies build advantage capabilities in fulfillment?

- They typically leverage a competitive advantage to manage suppliers and achieve economy of scale (e.g., Honda).
- They continually seek new ways to fulfill consumer needs and manage the entire supply chain (e.g., Dell Computer Corporation).
- They leverage supply-chain management to re-create business for new consumers or channels (e.g., GE).

Guaranteeing the Experience When Multiple Partners are Involved

In his book *The Only Thing That Matters*, author Karl Albrecht defines "any episode in which the customer comes into contact with the organization and gets an impression of its service" as a "Moment of Truth." As companies become increasingly virtual, it is becoming more and more likely that customers will experience moments of truth at the hands of agents. Agents can be individuals or businesses who are contracted to supply a specific aspect of service delivery to another company's customers. Such companies include: TeleTech, which handles diverse customer-care interactions via the telephone and Web for Global 1000 clients; Amazon.com, which handles the inventory management, order management, and fulfillment for the Toys "R"Us web business; or a smaller player such as R. E. Ricciardelli, Inc. which installs carpets on behalf of Home Depot for most of New England. In each of these cases, those delivering a moment of truth are not on the direct payroll of that company.

In the present economy, the drivers for such arrangements are numerous and can include: cost reductions, the absence of resources to build internal capabilities, the need to rapidly acquire operational capabilities and/or a global presence that would take far too long to grow internally, or an over-all desire to minimize risk and enhance operational flexibility. Most often, these third parties have built a core competency around the management and execution of a particular process, or they have established competency around doing business in a particular geographic or virtual location.

Whereas outsourcing arrangements have been long-standing in areas such as IT and the traditional outbound call center, they are becoming increasingly diverse, with entire processes or functions being outsourced to third parties. Of even greater significance is the fact that companies have realized how difficult it is to meet rising customer expectations at all customer touch-points. Busi-nesses such as Sears and Home Depot sell many "services" such as roof repair, appliance service, and carpet installation, but they outsource the execution of these services to third parties. Although these parties will most often identify themselves as being "from" the retailer when interacting with customers, they are not direct employees. Business-to-business context, outsourcing relation-ships that touch the customer are becoming more and more common in areas such as billing and collections, real-estate management, and recruiting. In order to make any of these relationships work, it is critical to manage the quality of the customer experience.

As the architects of the business model that ultimately delivers an "experi-ence" to customers, the primary vendor must define, design, implement, and then monitor the performance of the various processes that collectively deliver value to the customer. When third parties execute these processes, *Service Level Agreements* (SLAs) define the parameters of performance that the primary supplier must have for its business model to work. SLAs are contracts between service providers and customers. They define the services provided, the metrics associated with the services, acceptable and unacceptable service levels, liabilities on the part of the service provider and customer, and actions to be taken in specific circumstances.[1] SLAs are one of the few ways in which a primary supplier can ensure a quality customer experience when they cede control of moments of truth. SLAs frame the dialogue between business partners, allowing the relationship to be managed based upon fact rather than perception.

Whereas outsourcing can be a means of building a powerful service-delivery vehicle comprised of "best-of-breed" components, it also brings along related risk. Just as most companies would be wary about sole-sourcing a critical raw material, they must enter into outsourcing or service partnerships with even greater caution, as disentangling from these types of relationships can be complicated and actively maintaining a second source can be even more complicated.

In order to guarantee the customer experience, an SLA must address:

- A definition of the service provided, the parties involved, and the effective dates of the agreement.
- A specification of the hours and days during which the service or application will be offered, excluding time for scheduled testing maintenance or upgrades.
- Specification of the number and location of users and/or hardware for which the service or application will be offered.
- An explanation of how problems will be reported, including the conditions for escalating calls for help to higher levels of support. This should set an expected response time for problems.
- An explanation of procedures for requesting changes, possibly including expected times for completing routine requests.
- A specification of quality targets and explanations of how these metrics are calculated and how frequently they will be reported.
- Specification of charges associated with the service; maybe flat-rate or maybe tied to different levels of service quality.
- Specification of user responsibilities under the SLA (user training, maintaining proper desktop configuration, not introducing extraneous software or circumventing change management procedures).
- A description of the procedures for resolving service-related disagreements.[2]

Service Level Agreements should leave as little to chance as possible, and both parties should strive to make the agreement comprehensive and devoid of ambiguity. It is also important to note that, just as a company will want to modify its own business processes as its business requirements change, so will it want to change the processes covered by the service level agreement. SLAs must be "living" agreements with processes established to modify the services delivered. Once set in place, performance metrics tied to service level agreements should be integrated into the company's Balanced Scorecard. It is through active monitoring of these metrics that a capable company can ensure that the customer experience is being delivered in a manner consistent with the intent of the business architect.

Retaining and Leveraging Customers

Do your customers continue to do business with you and provide sources of leverage?

- Is your company viewed as a source of new products or services to the market?
- Does your company actively develop, promote, and sell new products?
- Does your company have a reputation of being the leader in new products?
- Do your customers purchase additional related products or services after the initial sale (is the greater percentage of your customers repeat customers)?
- Are you viewed as the market innovator?
- Is a full and current customer profile available at all times – do you amaze your customers with your knowledge of their needs?

Some companies score high on this test. Harley Davidson leverages relationships through its HOGs (Harley Owner Groups) to sell new products to current customers and build its customer base. GE leverages relationships among its companies to explore new business propositions (e.g., aircraft engines and leasing companies to lease airplanes).

How do companies like GE and Harley Davidson build advantage capabilities in retention and leverage?

- They leverage relationships to sell more products to their customer base (e.g., Home Depot).
- They leverage relationships to sell new products to current customers and build their customer base (e.g., Harley Davidson, Travelocity).
- They leverage relationships to explore new business propositions (e.g., AOL-Time Warner).

Maintaining State-of-the-Art Customer Management Capabilities

In their book *Customer Connections*, authors Robert Wayland and Paul Cole summarize the impact of technology on customer relationship management:

> Technology now permeates every aspect of the customer relationship, providing new and exciting possibilities for two-way, real-time conversation, collaboration, and commerce/care, delivered via a state of electronic conduits

including the Internet and intranet's self-service (e.g., kiosk) systems and mobile systems.

A major challenge facing companies today is "keeping up with the Joneses" when it comes to customer relations management. Once a customer experiences a great "moment of truth" with one company they come to expect the same service levels from other suppliers and providers. Often that experience is technology-enabled. For example, AT&T PersonalLink engaged Cambridge Technology Partners to build infrastructure that used open systems, and client/server technologies that incorporated computer-telephony integration to enable the system to capture data from incoming calls. The system uses this data to retrieve customer profiles from AT&T's customer database and displays the record on the customer service representative's (CSR) computer screen before the CSR picks up the phone. This computer-telephony technology also allows for dialed number identification. Knowing which number the customer called allows tailoring to specific services or even language preferences. CSRs can now provide custom services based on the caller's needs.[3]

Depending on business strategy, the capabilities required may be simple customer-interaction management solutions (computer, telephony, inbound voice, interactive voice response, outbound voice, and push technologies) or it may include chat, co-browsing, inbound e-mail handling, outbound e-mail, web-based training, and web callback. Increasingly companies are seeking more holistic e-CRM solutions that add marketing loyalty programs, transaction processing, and web support.

According to Ken Tuchman, CEO of TeleTech,

> Online customers expect service equal to or greater than what they've come to expect from traditional brick and mortar business. They also demand choices, including web and e-mail options and the ability to speak with a customer service agent in real-time. If customers don't receive the service they expect, the competition is just a click, phone call or street corner away. e-CRM is fast becoming a critical capability that leverages technology to facilitate communications with customers through properly structured voice, e-mail and Web interactions.

Companies must ask themselves the following questions as they relate to leveraging new opportunities:

- Are the distribution channels in my industry shifting to a consumer direct model?
- Are my technical systems and databases built around products rather than customers?

- Are my systems fragmented by diverse 800-numbers, e-mail addresses, departments, and functions?
- Am I leveraging opportunities and value of our customer relationships every time a customer contacts us?
- Do our customers enjoy high-quality interactions?
- Do our call centers generate more revenue than costs?

If the answers are unsatisfactory, companies must decide whether to build the capabilities themselves, source their technology from an Applications Service Provider (ASP), or outsource technology and staffing from an e-CRM company.

Upsell, Cross-Sell, and Leverage

Clayton Christensen, in his book *The Inventor's Dilemma*, has documented that when

> the best firms succeeded (in gaining customer input) they did so because they listened responsibly to their customers and invested aggressively in the technology, products and manufacturing capabilities that satisfied their customers' next-generation needs. But paradoxically, when the best firms subsequently failed, it was for the same reasons.

In short, the customer is not always right. As Frederick Reichheld put it:

> Companies should target the right customers, not necessarily the easiest to attract or the most profitable in the short term, but those likely to do business with the company over time.[4]

In addition to focusing on customers who are the most profitable, Capable Companies also pay attention to lead users of their products and services. Research suggests that identifying lead customers (i.e., early adopters of trends or technology) is a crucial step in innovation. As markets shift and technological advances quicken, companies must respond to opportunities, and better still, anticipate them. Lead customers/users have several characteristics important to companies. First, they foreshadow the general demand of the market. Second, they have a vested interest in the solution to the problem. Third, because of their experiences they can perceive and express needs more clearly. Fourth – and a real bonus – they often have prototype solutions. "Lead customers" often demonstrate these traits through participation in associations, user networks, customer advisory boards, and the like.

Companies should always have their sensing mechanisms turned on to listen to the voice of the customer. For example, opportunities can sometimes be found in the customer-attracting processes (e.g., the response to advertisements prompts new features) and almost always in the convert, fulfill, and leverage processes. These voices then become an ongoing stream of Change Forces that may require the company to act.

Customer Loyalty

Customer loyalty is a key issue for many companies today because existing customers are usually far more profitable than new ones. For example, according to Cognitor, increasing customer retention by 10 percent will generally equate a 50 percent increase in profits. Furthermore, attracting a new customer costs five times as much as selling to an existing one.[5] Customer retention therefore becomes a key indicator of future profitability.

The problem is that customer satisfaction is an imperfect measure for customer retention. It has been estimated that between 65 percent and 85 percent of customers who defect say they were satisfied with their former supplier.[6] Then why do customers defect?

Research suggests that customers defect for the following reasons:

- Deregulations allow new competitors (e.g., explosion of long-distance carriers).
- New competitors offer different value propositions (e.g., Amazon can ship directly to my house at a discount).
- A reduction in brand dominance (e.g., Xerox once was synonymous with "copy machine").
- The advent of new technologies (e.g., defections from the big financial houses to e-trading companies).

Capable Companies need sensing mechanisms to understand the impact of Change Forces to rapidly understand the gap between existing customer-relations-management capabilities and those needed in the near future.

Companies continually provide value when they are able to regenerate business through innovation. Customers do not remain loyal because of past customer satisfaction. They are more concerned with the ability of the company to meet their future needs. In other words, loyalty is earned by answering the question: "What can you do for me today and tomorrow?"

This represents a change in the thought process, from one that says "Let's do another customer satisfaction survey to see why customers defect" to one that gets companies to think more along the lines of "How do I read customer needs and track industry changes to anticipate changes in capabilities they expect in me?" By focusing on capabilities, companies turn their attention to process design and product or service enhancement.

The Building Blocks of the Capable Company

- Capable Companies understand CRM and recognize that it is not the responsibility of the sales force or some other department. Rather, CRM cuts across all company processes whenever the customer comes in contact with the company (directly or indirectly).
- Capable Companies focus on attracting the right customers to their value proposition.
- Capable Companies match capabilities to the customer-engagement method, whether that is in person, over the telephone, or over the Internet, to improve conversion rates.
- Capable Companies share customer information across the value-added chain to present one company to the customer.
- Capable Companies recognize the need for CRM capabilities and for the first time since the general ledger pay attention to keeping data current.
- Capable Companies pay attention to their customer information architecture.
- Capable Companies think about the CRM capabilities needed to support their value proposition and then make appropriate build, rent, or outsource decisions.
- Capable Companies understand that the key to customer loyalty is in the rapid and ongoing update of the company's capabilities.
- Capable Companies use advanced tools to learn from customers but recognize that the customer is not always right. They take time to understand the customer's needs or requirements and prioritize those requirements.
- Capable Companies routinely track the external environment for the Change Forces that will likely impact customer loyalty in the future.

Notes

1   http://www.onforum.com/tutorials/service_level/topic03.html
2   www.compuware.com

3   http://www.CTP.com/CTP_partners/att.html
4   Frederick F. Reichheld, "Loyalty-Based Management," *Harvard Business Review*, March–April 1993.
5   http://www.cognitor.com/cgpages/p7.html
6   Reichheld, "Loyalty-Based Management."

Part III   The Development and Alignment of Capabilities

If I had six hours to chop down a tree, I'd spend the first four sharpening the ax.

– Abraham Lincoln

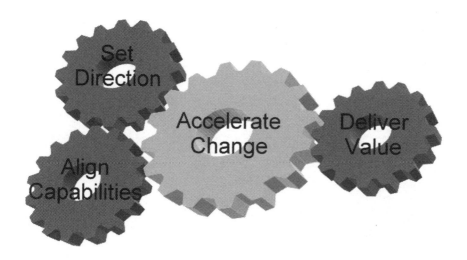

7 Architect Business Structure

Nothing astonishes men so much as common sense and plain dealing.

— **Ralph Waldo Emerson**

The Purpose of This Chapter

With strategy set and value-exchange mechanisms mapped out, the hard work of creating dynamic business architecture begins; one that can adapt and shed, balance adaptive vs. disruptive technologies, and minimize organization and technical complexity. We maintain that the development and alignment of capabilities requires a basic understanding of business architecture. This chapter serves as a primer on business architecture. We address architecture requirements in three areas: people, process, and technology, and present ways to think about keeping the architecture dynamic. In fact, we contend that the corporation's enabling systems are the key physical manifestation of its culture.

An architectural approach to business is not new, thanks to John Zachman and John Sowa's framework for *Information Systems Architecture* and David Nadler and Michael Tushman's *Organization Architecture*.[1] Business architecture design is a method for bringing critical corporate resources together to deliver value to customers and shareholders. Business and organization capabilities that translate strategy to action provide the shared point of alignment for all parties and provide a focal point for identifying the need for change to operational systems.

The Challenges

Business Architecture helps companies address the following challenges:

- Creating a dynamic architecture implies: the ability to adapt and shed, balancing adaptive vs. disruptive technologies, balancing organizational and technical complexity, and defining "best" in the context of a Capable Company.

- Balancing organizational and corporate structure with executive accountability and leveraging assets.
- Establishing a structure of accountability that encourages behaviors that contribute to the achievement of strategy.
- Organizing people to achieve results.
- Aligning people, process, and technology to essential business capabilities.
- Aligning IT and other systems to Business Strategy.

An Architecture Primer

Building designs begin with a series of conversations between an architect and those who understand how the building will be used. Architects listen to people describe what they will do inside the building, how they will communicate, how they will be organized, and what image of the company the owner wants to present. These conversations translate into an impression of the Purpose of the building, what its Mission will be, what is Valuable to the owner and inhabitants, the Processes that will be executed, and what people, information, and machine resources will provide the inhabitants with the Capabilities it needs to accomplish its mission. From all of this data, the architect creates a Vision and a Design for the building.

The design is documented in a set of architectural and engineering drawings that provide a highly structured view of the building from various points of view. The cover drawing is a site plan showing the surrounding area and defining the boundaries of the work site. Several elevation drawings provide a vision of the completed structure in its surroundings. Floor plans describe each level of the building, defining the locations of walls, utility shafts, and stairwells. Additional sets of drawings are provided to detail heating, ventilation, and air conditioning, electrical, plumbing, wall and floor treatments, and details for each of the contractors and trades that will be involved to realize the vision portrayed in elevation drawings. Often they include a three-dimensional or computer-based model of the building.

Using an iterative process of listening, creating, engineering, designing, and presenting, the architect arrives at a plan and a program that will result in a building being ready for use at a target cost and within a target schedule. The usefulness of the building depends entirely on the degree to which its structure and outfitting complement the way that the inhabitants of the company work within it. The long-term value of the building lies in its ability to be adapted to changes in the company's work and the way that it is done. The way that the components of a building come together and produce a serviceable space is called its architecture.

Similarly, the way that management, organization, policies, processes, finances, controls, and measures come together to produce business value can be referred to as business architecture. Just as with a building, a company's business architecture must fit and adapt to the company's work and ways of working to assure productivity and adaptability.

Changing Business *Archetypes*

At the beginning of the twentieth century, the driving factors of business architecture were geography, functional efficiency, and top-down direction. Organizationally, small numbers of educated people directed large numbers of people with focused skill sets to achieve functional efficiency. Typically, these companies relied on a militaristic command-and-control management style for clarity and coordination.

Geography was a dominant limiting factor and automation was a dominant productivity factor. As the twentieth century progressed, communications systems, trucking, and air transportation decreased the effect of distance, gradually reducing the limiting effect of geography and, at the same time, automation made the transition from competitive advantage to business necessity.

At the beginning of the twenty-first century, companies must operate globally, optimize their value-delivery processes, and rely on high levels of empowerment to compete. Twenty-first-century business competition is all about speed and efficiency. The function-and-features economy of the 1970s yielded to the quality economy of the 1980s, the service-experience economy of the 1990s, and the experience economy of the new millennium. The Internet arrived on the scene as a disruptive technology and smashed the communication and distance limitations of businesses, just as the elevator smashed the four-story limit at the beginning of the twentieth century.

Nadler and Tushman suggest four factors that contribute to new architectural designs. Purpose, for example the shopping mall, was designed to create a real-estate rental property that attracted retailers by allowing them lower rent and higher traffic. The stores in the mall are pretty much unchanged, but the setting is no longer the town square. In earlier chapters, we described Purpose, Mission, Vision, and Values as elements that define architectural purpose.

The second factor is structural materials, or the components that are available to the architect and with which the building can be constructed. In our mall analogy, the earliest malls had concrete paths, grassy areas, and open courtyards. New materials would be required to convert these malls into the enclosed "small communities" that we visit today. Similarly, the business and organization capabilities that a company has and needs are the structural materials of business architecture.

Architectural style is the third factor representing the creative and functional expression of purpose with structural materials. The enclosed mall and, in the extreme, the Mall of America, are expressions of architectural style, just like the underground malls in Paris and Montreal. Corporate Strategy, Business Focus, and Customer Value Proposition all establish the architectural style for a business.

Not all parts of a building contribute directly to appreciated value. Such elements as elevators, rest rooms, and fire-suppression systems represent the fourth factor and are referred to as collateral technology. Business architecture considers a similar set of infrastructure elements represented by information, human resources, and financial systems, to name a few. Table 7.1 describes the interrelationship among building and organization architecture factors.

Another business purpose would dictate a different set of architecture design factors, just as a sports complex would be built differently from a hospital. But here is where the analogy begins to break down. Occupants can move out of a building when it no longer serves their purpose. It is much more difficult to shed a business architecture and adopt a new one when the business purpose changes.

Table 7.1   Comparison of Building and Organization Architecture

Factor	Buildings	Organizations
Purpose	The function of the building (e.g., shopping mall).	Stimulate Product Innovation, emphasize Fast Time-to-Market and continually reduce Product Cost.
Structural Materials	Construction Materials (e.g., long-span roof trusses).	Teams, Collaboration, Empowerment
Architectural Style	The way materials are put together to create the building (e.g., enclosed mall).	Allied Corporate Strategy, Speed/ Innovation, Customer Value Proposition, and Collaboration as a dominant Organization Capability
Collateral Technology	Building elements that are needed even if not desired (e.g., parking lot).	Corporate Intranet, Knowledge Management, Company-Wide Leadership Development and Activity-Based Costing

Architecture Requirements

Dynamic business architecture is designed directly from operational strategy. In their book, *Competing by Design,* Nadler and Tushman compare three alternative operational designs. Each of the designs – traditional, process, and high-performance – is appropriate for some businesses and not for others. A manufacturing floor, operating room, or police force would operate better with a more "traditional" than "high-performance" design. "High-performance" designs are appropriate for customer-supporting and product-design operations of high-velocity companies. Choosing the most appropriate operational strategy components establishes a company's People Systems Architecture.

Many Operational Architectures could be developed from the 23 elements on the Operational Design Table shown in table 7.2.

Table 7.2 Comparing Designs

	Traditional	**Process Design**	**HPWS**
Point of View	Internally driven design	Design focused on customers and environment	
Degree of Clarity	Ambiguous requirements	Clear direction and goals	
Process Design Focus	Inspection errors	Control of variation at the source	
Design Life Cycle	Static designs dependent on senior management redesign	Capacity to reconfigure	
Work Group Intent	Highly controlled and rigidly separated units	Self-contained units	Empowered and autonomous units
Enabling Individuals	Limited information flow	Varying information flow	Broadened access to information
Job Definition	Narrowly defined jobs	Broadened but not necessarily enriched jobs	Shared, enriched jobs
Enabling the Organization	Technical system dominance		Integration of social and technical systems
Empowerment	Control-oriented management structures, systems, and culture		Empowering structures, systems, and culture
Human Resource Management	Controlling in restrictive human resource practices		Empowering human resource practices

Source: Adapted from David A. Nadler and Michael L. Tushman, *Competing by Design: The Power of Organizational Architecture* (Oxford University Press, 1997).

What is the right combination for a given company? It is the set that most closely enables the culture that fits a company's Purpose, Strategy, and Core Values. The process is straightforward:

1   Break down the Purpose, Strategy, and Core Value statements from paragraphs and sentences into "individual thoughts."
2   For each thought, consider each of the ten elements and options on the Operational Design Table.
3   Build an Operational Design Table or Operational Architecture from the elements and options that best fit the thoughts expressed in Purpose, Strategy, and Core-Value statements.

People Systems Architecture

People systems architecture addresses people, skills, roles, and projects, and consists of:

- Improving the selection of employees based on skills, roles, and availability.
- Providing employees with tools to participate in their career development.
- Improving the "line of sight" for both employees and managers.
- Increasing the ability to assemble, monitor, cancel, and redeploy assets in a timely manner.

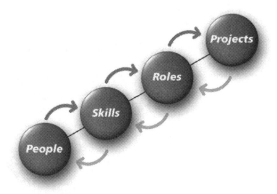

Figure 7.1   People Systems Architecture

When a good plan goes bad

Take the case of a thriving US-only machine-manufacturing company that was operating in a growing market but saw a plateau coming in the new millennium. Having anticipated a shift by its customers away from products manufactured with its machines to products manufactured with machines of an alternate technology, the decision was made to acquire several productive divisions of a competitor holding company, retool them, update product engineering, and enter the same market from a different direction. Two years after the acquisition, the three acquired businesses were still struggling to get back to their pre-acquisition levels of performance and customer satisfaction.

The acquisition plan called for the infusion of capital and know-how into three companies to achieve synergy and leverage. Unfortunately, each improvement drove the three companies further and further from their former business architecture. Three autonomous, family-operated companies were challenged to integrate into one, managed by an estranged cousin.

Essentially, the program was flawed in a dimension that had not been addressed during due-diligence or assimilation planning. The new parent wanted to turn three families into one machine and they did not want to change. Not only that, but employees and suppliers held allegiance to family members, not to their companies. Consequently, the supply chain broke down and essential knowledge left the company, leaving crippled production and customer-support capabilities behind.

Organizing people to achieve results

A high-tech manufacturing company performed a Change Readiness Assessment before implementing an Enterprise Resource Planning System. The examination revealed that the department with greatest overload level had the lowest stress level because it had the highest sense of alignment with business goals.

Employees of Capable Companies are competent in the skills required to do their jobs, are empowered to do what it takes to get their work done, and understand what business results will come from their work. These companies keep everyone focused on building or demonstrating capabilities through either executing value-adding Processes, Improving those processes, or creating new value-adding Processes.

Competency management is used to assure available skills. By examining Process and Technology Systems to establish skill- and competency-level requirements, then developing personnel development programs to build and maintain competency levels, these companies assure their ability to achieve their goals. This practice links personnel development back to strategy elements that drive the need for specific skills, which establishes a method for human resource development managers to plan and develop skills like other corporate resources.

Linking performance management to results

"Performance management" is a term frequently used in human resource and training circles, but it has many definitions. Some human-resource professionals use the term to mean a system for linking and maximizing individual, team, and organizational performance. Training professionals often use the term in the context of developing skills in line with the business strategy and nurturing and coaching the development of those skills. In some companies, performance management is no more than a simple scale or "factors system" used in performance appraisals. Other companies use the term synonymously with "performance appraisals," or define performance management as a "corrective process." Still others use it to cover a set of tools to "upgrade worker performance."

Capable Companies use the term in a broad context – a systematic approach to developing, strengthening, and reinforcing those actions required to maximize performance and organizational learning. In this context, performance management encompasses five domains:

1   Clear Strategy
    a   What are the implications of our corporate strategy?
    b   What are the implications of our business strategy?
    c   What are the implications of our value proposition to our customer?
    d   What key capabilities are needed for the future?
2   Clear Measures (individual and organizational)
    a   Do our performance measures help drive a balanced agenda?
    b   How do we develop a line of sight from the business unit through our core processes to work teams in individuals?
    c   How do we ensure accountability?
3   Rewards (financial and non-financial)
    a   How do we link rewards and incentives to key performance measures?
    b   Are alternative reward systems sufficiently present and/or properly designed to motivate and recognize both individual and group performance?
    c   How can rewards strengthen the commitment and retention of key contributors?
4   Development
    a   Are development plans linked to key performance measures?
    b   Are development plans linked to desired organizational capabilities?
    c   Do development plans help build employee commitment?
5   Feedback
    a   Do our systems provide clear feedback on how to improve employee, customer, and shareholder value?

b   How well are our 360-degree reviews accomplished?

c   Do our key leaders know how to give and receive feedback?

All five domains may enhance employee, customer, and shareholder value. Standards set for and by leaders should reflect values for these stakeholders. Standards may be set around behaviors (what leaders/employees do) and results (what they deliver), and rewards include financial short-term (bonuses, cash awards), financial long-term (stock grants, stock options, long-term incentives), and non-financial (recognition, the work itself). Feedback implies that managers know the score and track results by continually monitoring their performance against plan. Collectively, standards, measures, rewards, development, and feedback work together to establish a performance-management system to drive balanced stakeholder value.

Teamwork is neither team work nor collaboration

Another organization construct that Capable Companies employ with great success is Teaming. Capable Companies know the difference been Teamwork and Team Work. They associate the former with collaboration and mutual self-interest and they associate the latter with groups of people working together. This distinction should not be underrated. Capable Companies trust that individuals will work independently or together toward common goals, and that groups of people can work productively with diverse views and approaches being applied to a common issue. Capable Companies do not confuse teaming with responsibility, nor do they let employees confuse organization structure with empowerment or accountability.

A story has been told about a racing yacht whose crew represented the world's best at each position. Because the team was so good, it was decided that there would be no captain. Rather, the team would set strategy and run the boat collaboratively. As the story goes, the team failed miserably in its first races, and only when it appointed a captain from outside the crew did its performance reach the level of everyone's expectations. When interviewed, one of the crew said that a race is a series of thousands of decisions, each with a dozen options. At the end of each race twelve men and women got off the boat, remembering every decision they had called wrong. Each became crippled by indecision and deferred to the other until decisions were not getting made. When the captain took over, one person went home remembering thousands of decisions, some good and some bad, but showed up the next day with two jobs: make thousands of decisions and motivate the twelve-person crew to do what they do best.

Accountability structures

Another characteristic of Capable Companies is the ability of its people to make and meet commitments. Such companies have an acute sense of accountability that complements their acceptance of responsibility to get things done. Much of this results from clarity of goals, objectives, and boundaries of empowerment that enable freedom of judgment. That freedom is supported by the trust that all employees share goals and respect each other's commitments.

In such companies, commitment is a negotiated agreement between two or more parties where each commits to do work based on measurable results. Commitments are thoughtfully requested and made, they are continually managed, they are objectively assessed, and open feedback is provided to ensure positive results.

Empowering performance measurement systems and clear levels of authority to commit resources supports personal accountability and willingness to make commitments.

When companies attempt to increase velocity in their organizations, accountability structures often get in the way or create instability unless they are changed. E-procurement has been touted to enable companies to reduce their Maintenance, Repair, and Operational procurement costs by as much as 60 percent. One machinery manufacturer has achieved the same cost reduction by empowering its people with information, authority, and accountability, complemented by exception-reporting and periodic audits with open feedback.

It is clear that, from an architectural point of view, accountability structures are an integral part of the design of a Capable Company's operational architecture.

Process Systems Architecture

In 1987 John A. Zachman published his groundbreaking framework for the design of information systems architecture. In concept, it had the same basis as Nadler and Tushman's work and shared its simple elegance. The framework represents business operations in terms of the data that it uses in the processes that it executes across its network of operations. Data, Process, and Network establish the architecture design factors. Creating several views of each design factor, as shown in table 7.3, fleshes the framework out.

Process Architecture must enable the business and organization capabilities that enable the company to operate and produce value for customers and

Table 7.3 Process Systems Architecture

Element View	Data Description	Process Description	Network Description
Scope Description (Ballpark View)	List of entities important to the business	List of processes the business performs	List of locations in which the business operates
Model of the Business (Owner's View)	Entity/ Relationship Diagram	Functional Flow Diagram	Logistic Network
Model of the Information System (Designer's View)	Data Model	Data Flow Diagram	Distributed Systems Architecture
Technology Model (Builder's View)	Data Design	Structure Chart	System Architecture
Detailed Description (Out-of-Context view)	Database Description	Program	Network Architecture
Actual System	**Data**	**Function**	**Communications**

shareholders. Process Architecture answers the question: What processes do we need, how must they behave, and how must they be brought together to (a) enable Essential Organization Capabilities and (b) support Strategy?

In chapter 8 we shall describe how examination of a number of different companies, industries, and leadership styles in the context of this framework reveal that there are a number of archetypes, each of which can simplify Business Architecture design.

In 1992, John Zachman teamed up with John Sowa and extended the framework to incorporate People, Time, and Motivation as design factors. These additional columns are shown in table 7.4.

The extensions provided a valuable context for the design of information systems architecture, which we will extend even further here and in subsequent chapters.

Financial Systems Architecture

Financial Systems Architecture describes how revenue will be forecasted and generated, how spending will be planned and controlled, and how financial

Table 7.4   Process Systems Architecture – Extended

Element	People Description	Time Description	Motivation Description
Scope Description (Ballpark View)	List of organizations/ agents important to the business	List of events significant to the business	List of business goals/strategy
Model of the Business (Owner's View)	Organization Chart	Master Schedule	Business Plan
Model of the Information System (Designer's View)	Human Interface Architecture	Processing Structure	Knowledge Architecture
Technology Model (Builder's View)	Human/ Technology Interface	Control Structure	Knowledge Design
Detailed Description (Out-of-Context View)	Security Architecture	Timing Definition	Knowledge Description
Actual System	**Organization**	**Schedule**	**Strategy**

performance will be stated. A well thought-out and communicated Financial Architecture is critical to the design of overall business architecture. It establishes fundamental rules for financial accountability and auditability with which Process and Technology Systems must comply.

Often, Financial Architecture requirements are omitted from process and IT-system designs, causing them to fail or to cripple the company after implementation. One glaring example is the twin evil sins of Enterprise Requirements Planning System implementations. Inventory write-downs are almost inevitable when product- and inventory-costing methods become disconnected from pre-existing requirements. Similarly, Accounts Receivable and Days Sales Outstanding often blossom when Credit-Management and Invoice-Processing methods are changed without careful planning and impact forecasting.

Financial Architecture complements strategic objectives and business strategy by answering the question: What systems must be in place to forecast financial performance, set and achieve performance goals, and assure the integrity of financial controls and records? For the most part, Generally

Accepted Accounting Practices, Securities and Exchange Regulation, and other statutory mandates establish requirements for financial systems and therefore fundamental design principles for Financial Architecture. However, Operational Architecture and Strategy can demand an additional layer of audit or exception reporting to achieve the desired balance of control and empowerment.

Aligning IT to Business Strategy

The key issue for technology architecture is that it takes one and a half to two years to build technology infrastructure systems, and their useful life is about a year following deployment. In effect, IT systems must be designed for a future company in order to obtain a justifiable return on investment. The solution is to build technology systems with adaptable components and design technical architecture to support a range of business strategies.

Business Strategy is inherently future-oriented and in the best of cases, is accompanied by a set of alterative scenarios. Since technology architecture (information systems) can be designed directly from business strategy it is simple to keep them aligned. The Rosetta Stone that allows the translation of business strategy into IT strategy is the capability. When business strategy is stated as a set of business and organization capabilities, information technologists can use them as primary architecture and strategy design factors.

As such, Technology Architecture is designed to enable the future organization or, more appropriately, a number of future organization scenarios, each with a different complement of supporting business-process and data requirements. Capabilities, Processes, and Information Systems are tightly connected, albeit with different time frames. Whereas business capabilities can have a useful life of ten years or more, processes have a useful life of from six months to five years, with an average of less than one year, and IT systems have a useful life of from two to five years, with an average of just over two years.

Creating a Dynamic Architecture

In his book, *Managing at the Speed of Change*, Daryl Conner provides a metaphor for "the fear and anxiety within us all as we encounter the significant, unanticipated changes that shatter our expectations." He calls it "the Beast" and he tells us that if we are to succeed in making any great transformation, we must flush "the Beast" into the open and conquer it. Capable Companies prepare for the unexpected.

Hewlett Packard called continual organization change "Corporate Calisthenics." Reorganization, frequent process changes, continual process improvement programs, and managing balanced scorecards all enable companies to see change earlier and respond to it with less disruption. We refer to these as design elements of a dynamic architecture.

Many companies have fallen into the trap of using one design element as the total architecture. Such architecture surrogates include: Management by Objectives, Hoshin Planning, Continual Improvement, Business Process Engineering, Balanced Scorecards, and the Process-Centered Organization. Each of these design elements can only improve business performance if they do not violate the underlying architecture.

For example, a high-tech services company tried to transform itself into a process-centered organization in order to improve customer focus and collaboration and, at the same time, tried to implement an incentive–compensation program based on a Management By Objectives (MBO) model that did not allow cross-functional goals. Each program was crafted in isolation of the other, and unfortunately both required the commitment of the same individuals and supporting information systems. Such conflicting demands freeze organizations rather than empower them.

Peter Pyclik created the diagram in figure 7.2 to show how changes to the way people work relate to IT capabilities and architectures. Each column represents an organization improvement strategy. At the top of each column is the IT infrastructure required to best enable the strategy. For example: Teamwork is applied to improve efficiency and requires the support of messaging infrastructure.

Within each column, technical capabilities to the left of the arrow are paired with corresponding organization attributes to the right of the arrow. For example: Personal Mastery does not require Online Access but Shared Vision and Team Learning do. Finally, a line tied to each of the arrows interconnects the column tracks. The circles represent a company's score on the continuum. Therein lies the power of the model.

It is impossible for an organization to achieve Team Learning with only shared paper files, rewards for heroic service, core databases, and the inability to readily manipulate information. Think of the line as a slack rope: one score can move up or down over some distance without requiring the other to move, but the distance is limited and the consequence of too much stress is a broken system.

Pyclik's diagram is a remarkably simple explanation for three common organization-development and IT investment-failure modes:

1   Technology gets too far ahead of organization, causing poor ROI on the IT investment and "errors at the speed of light."

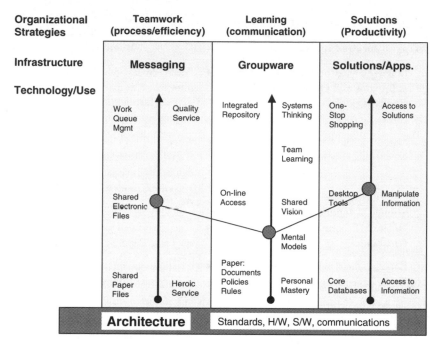

Figure 7.2   Work Styles and Enabling Technology

Source: Peter Pyclik, CIO, Boston Financial Systems.

2   Organization needs exceed technology capability, causing productivity roll-off and poor ROI on organization development investment.

3   Premature investment in IT lays in costly infrastructure that is grossly overpriced and underperforming, compared to available solutions in the future when the organization really needs them.

Balancing Organizational and Corporate Structure

The objective of building a Corporate Architecture from People, Process, Technology, and Financial Architectures is to bring all operational, governing, and measurement systems into alignment and to enable those systems to produce business value synergistically. There is a critical balance between Organizational and Corporate Structures that typifies the Capable Company. Capable Companies organize people using an architecture design approach. Table 7.5 illustrates a six-step process and the pitfalls each step helps to avoid.

It is the second and fourth steps that seem to trip up less Capable Companies. If processes are organized to support functions rather than to execute

Table 7.5   Six Steps to Organization Alignment

Steps to Aligned Action	Benefits
1 Define Strategy and state it in terms of Business and Organization Capabilities.	• Avoid having your Strategy interpreted in many different ways and translated into a hodgepodge of Capabilities.
2 Manage a set of Capabilities to deliver Business Value.	• Keep executive attention on Capabilities allows them to avoid details of implementation and empowers those who must deliver them.
3 Organize Processes to realize Capabilities.	• Keep Processes focused on Strategy-enabling Capabilities.
4 Establish measures to enable Performance Management.	• Maintain the focus of performance management on what is most important.
	• Avoid process improvement beyond the level of necessary performance.
5 Organize Work Teams to execute Processes.	• Aligning People to Process, appropriate numbers of people and proper skill sets can be readily identified and managed.
6 Organize management to optimize Work Teams.	• Build, support, and focus Work Teams to maximize process and in turn Capability effectiveness and efficiency.

capabilities, they become misdirected. For example: one company's Risk-Management group focused on financial-cost minimization rather than on Customer Value Management Process performance, resulting in gradual erosion of response capability. The proper business-value objective was not apparent. Similarly, we see process or functional experts put into positions where their ability to grow and motivate people is often less well developed than performance improvement goals demand.

The Building Blocks of the Capable Company

- Capable Companies link all their operational systems to their business strategy through a set of business and Organization Capabilities.
- Capable Companies align their People, Process, Technology, and Financial Systems to deliver or demonstrate Business Capabilities.
- Capable Companies design architectures for People, Process, Technology, and Financial Systems that establish minimum requirements and describe how the various elements will interoperate.
- Capable Companies pay particular attention to their Organization Structure, Accountability, and Competence of Employees to assure their ability to deliver value to customers and stakeholders.
- Capable Companies embed financial controls and performance measures into all their systems.
- Capable Companies define their strategy in terms of their business and organization capabilities.
- Capable Companies focus on process management, not functional management.
- Capable Companies organize themselves and equip their managers to form high-performance work teams.

Note

1 John A . Zachman, "A Framework for Information Systems Architecture," *IBM Systems Journal*, 28, 3 (1987) and David A. Nadler and Michael L. Tushman, *Competing by Design: The Power of Organizational Architecture* (Oxford University Press, 1997).

8 Align Capabilities

The attainment of the carpenter is that his work is not warped, that the joints are not misaligned, and that the work is truly planed so that it meets well and not merely finished in sections.

– Miyamtoto Musashi

The Purpose of this Chapter

This chapter addresses the implications of various business archetypes on business architecture. For example, whether your corporate strategy seeks a high degree of synergy among its businesses or firewalls between them matters to capability development. Based on the choices made, certain capabilities fit better than others. Having a framework helps to identify early in the game the red flags that should be raised and the warning signals that should sound when trying to put a square peg in a round hole. In this chapter, we provide a case study to illustrate alignment problems that cause organization friction. Left untreated, alignment problems waste energy. We conclude with a method to align process, technology, and organization proactively.

On Nantucket Island off the coast of Massachusetts, USA, there is a peculiar house called "Sans Souci." The name has a double meaning. French for "without care," it refers not only to a vacation spot but also to how the house was put together. Made from various parts of shipwrecks, a boathouse, and parts of a twine factory, no two of the home's windows are alike. While making Ripley's Believe It Or Not list of oddities, the charming house is not without its challenges: floors and ceiling are not aligned, there is no consistent style, and it's hard to upgrade.

The Challenges

When building a new company, the initial design is likely to have a high degree of integration of essential components geared to product development.

However, as companies grow and mature, they undergo changes in management, board members, markets, and strategy. They are left with a mishmash of archetypes made up of management styles, organization structures, and process designs. Soon they start looking more and more like the Sans Souci house. Contributing factors include:

- Rapid changes in technology and business process require a consistent disciplined approach, yet companies do not have an enterprise-wide strategy.
- Incorrect decisions are made because current reality didn't take into account predictable future events.
- Companies are constrained in the execution of their business plan by past business capability choices.
- Multiple "best-in-class" solutions are found to interfere with each other after deployment.

Unlike the builders of the Sans Souci house, an architect will explore several aspects of what the structure will be used for and who will use it before putting pencil to paper. These two questions are often given short shrift when designing companies and the result can be disjointed in the long run. Architects know that certain structure types and layouts work better than others for a given purpose and they therefore winnow down the possibilities to one of several typical structures before exploring the details.

It is easy to visualize the difference between a personal residence and a sporting complex and then explore various different types of personal residences to get to the exact requirements for a given client. Architects reference six to ten basic personal residence styles as *archetypes* and have given them names that are usually quite recognizable, such as Garrison Colonial, Cape Cod Ranch, Salt Box, or Contemporary. Once the architect finds a connection between the client's view of the structure and one of the archetypes, the next phase of exploration begins.

Setting the archetype aside, the architect explores who will live in the house. How many people? What is their lifestyle? What is their future desire for their lifestyle and the house? Will there be pets? A housekeeper? Because architects know that certain client choices will drive specific design paths, those questions are asked early in the process:

- How many people? – water supply, waste water, bedrooms, baths, cars...
- Do you entertain? – dining, parking, public space, closets...
- Will you have a pool? – perimeter control, cabana, flooring material...

From these elements, the architect defines a purpose for the structure, a strategy for using space, goals for key activities that will take place in and around the home, and preliminary elements of style that will be used for the detailed design. Within the boundaries of the main structure, say a Garrison Colonial with a pool and three-car garage, the architect begins to apply another layer of archetypes, including home office/garage, master-bedroom suite, entertaining kitchen/dining area and pool/cabana to build out a preliminary design for review. The use of archetypes accelerates the process and assures the interoperability of the individual components.

Companies face a similar set of challenges when they design or reengineer their businesses. They must make sure that the various components that they bring together to build their company will interoperate efficiently and effectively. Too often, companies trust best practices to be useful archetypes.

The Problem with Best Practices

Best Practices are only "best" in a given setting and can be significantly less than optimum when wedged together. Our Sans Souci house is a physical example. The parts taken from shipwrecks and used in its construction were "best-practice" components of the ships that they came from, but barely useful parts of a home.

In the late 1970s many people worked hard to build energy-efficient homes. Over several years, a large collection of best practices emerged, including solar water-heaters, airtight wood stoves, six-inch stud walls, R-30 roofing insulation, and foam wall insulation. Although each element was "best," when they were brought together into a single home, they created a maintenance-riddled "sick home" that failed to breathe, trapped moisture, and was impossible to keep at a comfortable temperature except when all the windows were left open.

A report by The Conference Board tells us:

> Many corporations have moved towards a management model characterized by decentralization, empowerment, and devolution of the business into self-governing entities. Others have embraced integration initiatives, which help hold a large corporation together...both research and anecdotal evidence reveal that CHQ-led [Central Headquarters-led] collaboration initiatives result in an unusually high level of frustration and disappointment, often realizing only partial success or ending in outright failure.[1]

The report goes on to suggest that the allied model is the most workable strategy for global competitiveness. In operation, allied is the most complex and difficult to manage of the three corporate strategy models. Does every global competitor need high complexity? In chapter 4, we described the factors that guide the selection of this element of a company's strategic choices.

When we think about our customer value proposition, should we focus on Customer Price, Quality, Speed, Service, or Innovation? All of them? What mix? In chapter 4 we described the set of goals that drive this choice, and a method for narrowing down the list of areas were best practices should be applied to maximize return on shareholder value. Clearly, not everything needs to be "best," but elements that need to be better than those of competitors should be driven to world-class status by studying the way those who are the best get it done.

Performance benchmarking is a very effective way of establishing goals for those elements where world-class performance is needed. However, benchmarking must be executed in the context of performance goals, overall company architecture, and similar advantage capabilities.

A frequent benchmark study error is choosing target companies in only the same industry as one's own. It is more desirable to choose companies with similar advantage capabilities. For example, a broadband cable company that chose superior service and broad offerings as its differentiators found that timely, accurate billing with multiple payment methods was the number-one desire of its customers. The company did not look to other cable companies. Rather, it benchmarked against several of the top telephone companies who were successfully leveraging very capable billing systems.

Organization Archetype Implications

Context was listed as an important element of benchmarking and choosing goals and/or solutions for equipping a company with its complement of capabilities. There are three elements that come together to create a context for examining capability solutions: organization, processes, and technology. As we described in chapter 7, all three work together to create capabilities that do what the company wants done in the way that the company wants them done. If there are interoperation difficulties, capability will be limited and business performance will suffer.

As we walk through a number of business architecture choices, we will use an example that is probably all too familiar to the reader. We will examine the synergies and conflicts between a decision to implement an Enterprise Resource Planning (ERP) system and various strategy, capability, and goal choices. As we proceed through this chapter, we will fill out a table that we refer to as an Architecture Fit Matrix (table 8.1).

Table 8.1 Architecture Fit Matrix Template

Characteristics of the selected ERP system	Architectural Impacts		
	Business Process	Information Technology	Organization
X			
Y			

The matrix is used as part of a large-scale IT-deployment failure diagnosis. The partial matrix that we shall build very closely resembles one that was constructed to analyze a very well-known ERP project at a high-technology company. However, many will see parallels to their own experience with Customer-Relationship Management, Sales-Force Automation, and other information systems.

In the second column of table 8.1, the attributes of the IT system under study are listed. For a full-scale ERP package, this may create more than 5,000 rows to begin with, but reduce to several hundred that truly drive business value and/ or describe desired synergies and threatening conflicts. The next three columns describe the impact of each attribute as it relates to Business Process, IT, and Organization Capability Architectures. See table 8.2, for example.

Table 8.2 Architecture Fit Matrix – ERP Example

Attributes of the selected ERP system	Architectural Impacts		
	Business Process	Information Technology	Organization
Shared and enforced business rules facilitate a high degree of coordination/ collaboration	**Rule variations for unique requirements are costly and slow to implement**	Business-rule changes will propagate simultaneously and immediately to all processes	*Demands a cross-functional process management orientation*
Shared customer information base with complete sales and service history	Each of the three sales entities will have access to all customers to provide service and support	Two customer-support systems will be integrated with the new ERP system to maintain data integrity	Customers can be readily shared across the three sales units and eight service centers

Cells in bold indicate a direct conflict between the ERP capability and the way that the company has chosen to organize and/or work. Cells in italic indicate a caution where additional cost or a higher risk of success is present. Normal text indicates a neutral or positive capability match.

Choices made by the company about its Corporate Strategy, Business Focus, Customer Value Proposition and Organization Capabilities will determine if the ERP attribute supports, or is in conflict with the desired business choices.

Corporate Strategy

Business architecture must be designed from what a company will do and how it wants to work. Let's examine the impact of Corporate Strategy Choice (introduced in chapter 4) on systems deployment.

If a company is to operate as a federation of allied divisions, there is a need for collaboration among people in the various divisions to leverage shared services and to exchange information at a detailed level. An integrated enterprise will benefit from each of these system requirements to a greater degree, and a holding company will require very little, if any, of this detailed-level collaboration. Table 8.3 describes some of the systems implications of Corporate Strategy archetypes.

What would happen if a company with a holding company Corporate Strategy chose to implement an integrated suite of business applications such as SAP R/3 or Oracle without extensive customization? In effect, the company will have chosen to implement the same system once for each division and once for its corporate head office, yet perhaps providing none of them with a good fit between its business processes and the technology used to automate them. Worse still, it will have adopted a single strategy for how people will work across all divisions by selecting a single process-automation model. More than one company has felt the pain of ineffective business execution caused by bad fit among people, process, and technology.

What if the same company chose a single installation for all companies? This would be represented in our matrix as what we see in table 8.4, where the bold text would indicate places where the Holding Company Strategy is violated.

Corporate Strategy Drives Corporate-Level Capabilities

Another element of context can be derived from a clear picture of how important various capabilities will be to a company given its corporate strategy choice. Although at any point in time certain capabilities such as "Acquisition Due Diligence" may change to become very important, companies often become distracted by thinking that they must do everything with the same

Table 8.3   Corporate Strategy Archetypes

Corporate Strategy Component	Integrated (McDonald's)	Allied (HP)	Holding (Tyco International)
Business Strategy	A single set of advantage capabilities → a single set of enabling systems	Multiple sets of advantage capabilities → multiple sets of interconnected enabling systems	Multiple sets of advantage capabilities → multiple sets of enabling systems
Customers	Same customers → systems enable a single view of customer engagements	Shared customers → systems enable a single view of customer engagements across the enterprise and maintain separate customer information-management systems within each company	Different customers → systems maintain single view of customer engagements within each company
Corporate Role	Set priorities among capabilities and detail a broad set of standard systems	Set priorities among capabilities; establish a narrow set of standard systems and coordinate a broader set of localized systems	Set goals or guidelines for systems
Human Capital	Maintain each set of systems through one set of organizations with cross-functional goals	Maintain lead organizations at corporate level and establish centers of expertise with cross-functional goals throughout the enterprise	Maintain each set of systems through one set of organizations in each company
Systems	Monolithic or highly integrated	One or more suppliers providing one or more configurations of a single product linked at the business transaction level	One or more suppliers providing one or more configurations of a single or multiple products communicating summary information to a set of corporate systems
Enabling Processes	Lead management and core team co-located with enabling facilities. Team members distributed close to advantage and strategic support work	Lead management and core team co-located with enabling facilities. Team members distributed close to advantage work and strategic support work is brought to the core team	Lead management and core team co-located with enabling facilities. Team members distributed close to advantage and strategic support work plus duplicate systems located and managed at the corporate business unit

Table 8.4   Architecture Fit Matrix – Holding Company Example

Attributes of the selected ERP system	Architectural Impacts		
	Business Process	**Information Technology**	**Organization Capabilities**
Shared and enforced business rules facilitate a high degree of coordination/ collaboration	**Rule variations for unique requirements are costly and slow to implement**	**Business-rule changes will propagate simultaneously and immediately to all processes**	**Demands a cross-functional process management orientation**
Shared customer information base with complete sales and service history	**Each of the three sales entities will have access to all customers to provide service and support**	*Two customer-support systems will be integrated with the new ERP system to maintain data integrity*	**Customers can be readily shared across the three sales units and eight service centers**

degree of excellence and control. This distraction dilutes resources, especially executive attention.

In this first grouping (see table 8.5), growth and contraction capabilities are linked to what the company chooses to do, while communications control and policy-setting capabilities are driven by how the company must operate.

Table 8.5   Corporate Strategy Drives Corporate-Level Capabilities

	Integrated Company	Allied Company	Holding Company
Acquisitions		SS	A
Employee Communication	BN	A	SS
Franchising	A	SS	
Internal/External Communications	A	A	SS
Management/ Operations/Policy/Leadership	A	A	SS
Mergers	A	SS	SS

Key: A = Advantage, SS = Strategic Support, BN = Business Necessity.

Many integrated and allied companies fail to establish effective protocols for Management, Operations, Policy Setting, and Leadership, resulting in constrained anarchy. Capable Companies with integrated or allied strategies excel in the ability of their executive and senior management teams to identify areas where synergy and difference exist. They also effectively collaborate to develop and execute business practices that at best are shared, frequently complement each other, and rarely conflict.

Table 8.6 Architecture Fit Matrix – Integrated Company Analysis

	Architectural Impacts		
Attributes of the selected ERP system	**Business Process**	**Information Technology**	**Organization**
Corporate organization structure and chart of accounts can be extended almost indefinitely	New businesses can be readily integrated into the process stream and new streams can be built and integrated as well	*Acquired businesses must be rapidly migrated to the ERP system. Interface technology will be of little value except in migration of data*	Training program development and execution with short-term coaching by application experts will be critical
Customer, product, project, and financial account numbers may be assigned at the lowest level of transaction detail	Existing transaction sets and processes can be used for acquired entities	*Historical financial, sales, product, and project data may have to be transformed to new structures to enable trend analysis*	Information sharing will be seamless

Our subject company chose an Integrated Corporate Strategy. It chose to build its initial set of Advantage Capabilities by merging the capabilities of a number of its suppliers with its own. Our matrix would display the impact of these choices (see table 8.6).

Note: Consider the same chart for an allied company Corporate Strategy. There would be a few conflict (bold) cells.

Strategy Drives Advantage-Capability Emphasis

Tables 8.7 to 8.13 suggest some implications of the choices outlined in the previous chapters. In each section, we have examined the typical publicly held

Table 8.7 Organization Capability Focus

	Organization Capability			
	Learning	**Speed**	**Boundarylessness**	**Accountability**
Balanced Scorecard	A	A	A	A
Budgeting	SS		SS	A
Contracting and Outsourcing		SS	A	SS
Employee Evaluation	A	SS	SS	A
Employee Suggestions	A	SS	A	BN
Goal Setting	SS	A	A	A
Planning	A	SS	A	SS
Public Relations	BN	BN	SS	BN
Rapid Change		A	SS	
Strategic Planning	A	A	A	A
Telecommuting			SS	SS

Table 8.8   Architecture Fit Matrix – Impact on Organization Capabilities

Attributes of the selected ERP system	Architectural Impacts		
	Business Process	**Information Technology**	**Organization**
HR competency modeling and evaluation provides 360-degree instrument processing	Current ad hoc performance management methods can be standardized	Network security will become a SS capability	*A performance management program will be developed and a three-cycle transition period will be disruptive*
Integrates transaction data, flow rates, counts, and delays across all applications and provides drill-down access via a scorecard of balanced measures	**A significant amount of manual effort and most time lags will be eliminated from the performance measurement programs**	*There will be an initiative to set new measures and the transaction systems will require attention to automate collection, summary, and presentation*	MBO and Six-Sigma programs can be enabled through new measurement capabilities.

company and created a family of business archetypes that can be used as a starting point for detailed systems design. The lists are not comprehensive, but they are representative of a large set of capabilities and the various choice drivers. In each table, A denotes Advantage Capability, SS denotes Strategic Support Capability, and BN denotes Business Necessity Capability.

Table 8.7 shows how the business value of some common business capabilities would vary with choices of Organization Capabilities.

Notice how the simple capability "Employee Suggestions" takes on different value with Organization Capability emphasis. A learning organization must have open and structured communications around a shared set of goals. At the same time, employee suggestions contribute less to Speed and little to Accountability.

There are two ways to use this data with our ERP system analysis. First, focus evaluation and assessment of fit to Advantage and Strategic Support Capabilities, and don't pay anything for Business Necessity or unnecessary ERP system capabilities.

Second, a few capabilities show up as alerts in the matrix in table 8.8 for an organization that is focusing on Learning and Accountability.

When a company chooses its Business Focus, the value of many common business capabilities can be ranked according to their contribution to business value. Often, this is the area where Best Practices implementation programs create more conflict than efficiency. For all but very few companies, the business capabilities listed in the first column of table 8.9 will never be more than Business Necessities. When selecting technologies, don't pay for product features that will yield little additional business value.

Table 8.9 Business Focus and Support Services

	Business Focus				
	Product/ Service	Customer/ Market	Technology	Production	Distribution
Accounting	BN	BN	BN	BN	BN
Cost Controls/Measuring	BN	BN	BN	BN	BN
Debt/Credit Collection/ Management	BN	BN	BN	BN	BN
Document Control/ Records Management	BN	BN	BN	BN	BN
Environment/Health/ Safety	BN	BN	BN	BN	BN
Finance	BN	BN	BN	BN	BN
Payroll	BN	BN	BN	BN	BN
Recycling/Waste Management	BN	BN	BN	BN	BN
Regulations	BN	BN	BN	BN	BN

Capabilities Driven By Customer Value Proposition Choices

When a company chooses among options for creating its competitive advantage, it also sets the stage for a complement of systems capabilities. For example: A startup cable network company built a very strong business plan based on proven elements from several successful companies and adaptations of proven concepts from completely disconnected industries. When the plan was examined and translated into a set of process (how we conduct business), organization (how we behave), and technology (how we enable our processes and organization) capabilities, a few things became clear:

- Technology that was currently available for integrated voice, data, audio, and video services would provide a strong competitive advantage at a lower operating cost than the company's competitors.
- Competitors' customers were crying out for better service attentiveness and dreaded dealing with up to three seemingly warring companies under a single name when they needed assistance.
- Most competitors suffered from weak billing systems that resisted change.

Analysis of the capabilities indicated a shift in strategy from being a low-cost provider to being a highly responsive single source of communications services at a premium price. In the process of taking strategy to action, the company discovered a new and stronger strategy. Success relied on being able to capitalize on technology for both business operations and product delivery and on selling the new strategy to investors. This is an extreme example of technology-driven business change used to exaggerate the need for rapid response to change forces from within and outside the company.

An integrated voice, data, audio, and video service infrastructure was indeed the company's product offering. However, service and speed of delivery (provisioning services to the household or business) had become the company's differentiating capabilities. To support the new strategy, IT systems such as our client's billing and call-center systems would be built to support rapid provisioning and accurate, integrated billing. In effect, system choices were driven as much by how the company had chosen to work as it was by what it had chosen to do. Synergy across people, process, and technology systems maximized the value of investments in each.

Table 8.10 is a partial list of business capabilities ranked in value for each of the five Customer Value Proposition choices described in chapters 4 and 5.

Table 8.10 Business Capabilities Ranked by Customer Value Proposition

	Customer Value Proposition				
	Price	Quality	Speed	Service	Innovation
Service Management	SS	A	A	A	SS
Configuration Management		A	BN	A	
Service Provisioning		A	A	A	
Failure Analysis /Measuring/ Monitoring		A	BN	SS	
ISO, QS...		SS		SS	
Product Performance Measurement/ Iimprovement	BN	SS	BN	A	
Process Performance Improvement/ Management	A	SS	A	BN	
Quality Assurance	BN	A	BN	SS	
Quality Improvement		A		SS	SS
Reliability		A	BN	SS	SS
Repair	BN	BN	BN	A	BN
Testing		BN	SS	SS	
Warranty	A	SS		SS	SS

Considering the high-technology company's choice to compete on speed and service, the assessment matrix might look like table 8.11.

Table 8.11 indicates a few areas where complexity will be greater than desired and one area where the IT people who support Provisioning will be required to know two significant business applications that operate on different platforms. The add-on product will impact recruiting, retention, training, and compensation.

Table 8.11   Architecture Fit Matrix – Implications of Speed and Service

| Attributes of the selected ERP system | Architectural Impacts | | |
	Business Process	Information Technology	Organization
Central and technician dispatch – wired and wireless	Field technicians self-dispatch, close customer orders, and authorize billing	*Wireless networking product will be used for all field-service communications*	Technicians will be empowered to satisfy the customer and serve the investor
Flexible billing engine integrates contract, ad hoc and service invoicing transactions	Customers will receive a single invoice for all services provided within 12 hours of a service period close	Infrastructure will be provided to 99.999% availability and 4-hour billing process-run service levels	All service provisioners and providers will work together to assure customer satisfaction
Serialized product control add-on from third-party provider	Customer Premise Equipment (CPE) will be sold or rented and services will be tied to CPE serial numbers	*Tailored integrated applications will be used to avoid integration and interoperability issues*	IT staff will be capable of managing all aspects of integrated systems that support a business process

Aligning People, Process, and Technology Proactively

Over time the friction caused by lack of fit causes heat in the organization, slows the organization down, and throws it off track. Like a misaligned automobile, or a house flunking inspection, the reasons behind the alignment problem are not always visible unless you know where to look.

During a study of companies who had suffered major IT initiative failures, one company avoided disaster by recognizing that their Customer Value Proposition would not be supported by their choice of an ERP planning system. Specifically, Dell Computer was well into an ERP deployment when it recognized that the track that they were on would complement their desire for Collaboration and Information Velocity, but that it would hinder the attainment of Speed goals with respect to having a highly adaptable manufacturing operation.

At one of their Platinum Council meetings where Dell executives meet with key customer account CIOs, Kevin Rollins, Dell's Vice-Chairman, talked about the critical need for every aspect of the company to be capable of changing its process rapidly. He referred to this as an essential part of what he called *velocity*, or the continuous speeding-up of every business process. At that same meeting, Michael Dell described his business as being a virtually integrated system of processes and products, extending from suppliers through

Dell's manufacturing and distribution processes, on to end customers, and the support of the product on their desktops. He also talked about the company's distributed management style and how continuous process improvement was a way of life throughout the company.

Following a discussion with several members of the executive team, the following segment of one of our matrices was created (table 8.12). In fact, these conversations triggered the design of a capability-based IT-selection process and the assessment method that has been shown here.

The chosen ERP solution certainly provided zero-latency data-availability, and it promised seamless integration and less complexity. However, other traits of the solution would have limited the ability of the company to manage processes in a distributed manner, violating the company's management and process improvement style. As shown in table 8.12, had Dell's Business Capabilities been mapped against the Capabilities of the ERP system, two strong cautions would have been raised. This would have taken place even before potential suppliers were engaged and well before any large expenditure had been made.

A broad set of capabilities are driven by the choice of business strategy. Once a company has chosen its competitive differentiators, a large set of capabilities can be ranked to establish their relative importance to the successful execution of strategy. It is this area where many companies make confused decisions by basing them on intuition and previous job experience rather than by thoughtful application of Types of Work and architecture design.

Table 8.12 Architecture Fit Matrix – ERP Implications

| Attributes of the selected ERP system | Architectural Impacts | | |
	Business Process	Information Technology	Organization
Predefined business functions prescribe organization structure	Work architecture must map directly to transaction definitions	*Reporting systems that infer organization structure from business functions will need adjustment*	**It is costly to adopt prescribed business function models**
Integrated transactions and functional modules demand users who are task-and context-skilled	Impact of zero-latency and zero propagation time must be designed into processes	Data consistency highly determined by workflow configurations	Workers will learn the upstream and downstream implications of their transactions
Shared and enforced business rules facilitate a high degree of coordination/ collaboration	**Rule variations for unique requirements are costly and slow to implement**	Business-rule changes will propagate simultaneously and immediately to all processes	Demands a cross-functional process management orientation

Also, this is the area where Best Practices programs can create more conflict than efficiency. As each constituency tries to build world-class capability for their areas of responsibility, Business-Necessity and Strategic Support capabilities can get too much attention and investment. Often, striving for "the best in everything we do" creates a behemoth of a solution that cannot be delivered in a timely or cost-effective manner.

Having experienced this in a previous ERP program, the CEO of a large multinational plastic parts-production machinery manufacturer engaged the services of a consulting firm to help it select a replacement ERP system for six of its manufacturing divisions. The company had committed itself to lean manufacturing and Six Sigma quality for all of its business operations – two programs that would consume 10 percent of its executive and senior management's attention for a seven-month period.

The CEO provided initial guidance to find the one system that all could use and to focus on shop-floor inventory control. After only a few days of examination, it was determined that there were two dominant Customer Value Propositions in play, each of which demanded a different set of Advantage Capabilities. The divisions who were focused on technology innovation and who sold through distributors demanded much stronger CRM and Collaborative Engineering capability. The divisions who sold directly to end customers and leverage Production Capacity did not share the need for collaborative engineering. Consequently, there was not one solution; but there were at least two.

Table 8.13 is a partial list of business capabilities ranked in value for each of the five business strategy choices described in chapter 4. Notice the difference in value assigned to various capabilities that would be used by this company with both Technology- and Production-focused divisions.

> **The power of Business Archetypes lies in the way that a few decisions thoughtfully made can suggest answers to many questions and lower-level solution archetypes. When strategy is stated in terms of the capabilities, ambiguity is removed from solution requirements and ultimately leads to better choices.**

Here we have applied this to IT, but the method is equally applicable to Human Resources, Financial Management, and other enabling capabilities that every company must have. Furthermore, the tables may be extended with additional choices and capabilities by considering what your company wants to get done and how it wants to do it.

The basic decisions are clear, as are the choices. Thoughtful consideration of People, Process, Technology, and Finance capabilities in the context of any company's strategy for success can enable rapid selection and prioritization of requirements for enabling systems.

Table 8.13 Ranking Business Capabilities

	Business Focus				
	Product/ Service	Customer/ Market	Technology	Production	Distribution
Activity-Based Costing	SS	SS		SS	SS
Asset Management	A	A	BN	A	BN
Complaint Handling	A	A	BN	SS	A
Customer Requirements	A	A	A	BN	A
Customer Satisfaction	A	A	BN	SS	A
Customer Service	A	A	BN	SS	A
Customer Training	A	A	A		
Delivery/ Distribution/ Freight/Logistics	SS	SS		SS	A
Employee Benefits/ Compensation/ Incentive Programs	BN	BN	SS	BN	BN
Employee Retention/ Turnover	BN	BN	SS	BN	BN
Engineering	SS	SS	A	BN	
Information Systems/ Technology	SS	SS	A	SS	BN
Inventory/ Warehousing Management	BN	BN		A	A
Knowledge Management		A	A		
Manufacturing/ Assembly	SS	SS	SS	A	
Product/Service Delivery	A	A	BN	SS	A
Product Design	SS	A	A		
Product Development	SS	A	A		
Product Management	A	SS	A		
Project Management	SS	SS	A	SS	SS
Research and Development	SS	A	A		
Self-Directed Teams			A		

In subsequent chapters we shall describe methods for sensing the need for changes to capabilities and responding to them rapidly.

The Building Blocks of the Capable Company

- Capable Companies are designed, not thrown together, by well-intentioned and knowledgeable people working independently with different interpretations of strategy.
- Capable Companies adapt best practices to their Advantage and Strategic Support capabilities. They do not adopt those of others with different agendas.
- Capable Companies make thoughtful decisions about how to organize, measure, and enable business processes.
- Capable Companies recognize that the value of their capabilities is directly tied to strategic choices.
- Capable Companies know that synergy among capabilities creates competitive advantage.
- Leaders of Capable Companies understand how investments in capabilities will enable or hinder execution of strategy.

Note

1   The Conference Board, *Organizing for Global Competitiveness*, Research Report 1291-01-RR.

Part IV Accelerating Change

Strategy is the evolution of a central idea over continually changing circumstances.

**– Helmuth von Moltke,
nineteenth-century Prussian general**

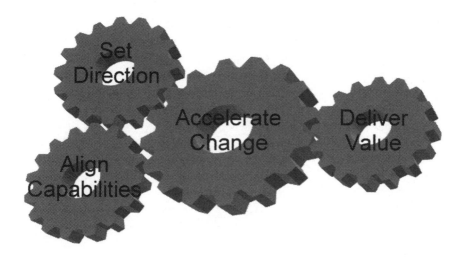

9 Track a Moving Target

Deprived of information one cannot assume responsibility, but given the information one cannot avoid responsibility.

– Eugene Taurman

The Purpose of This Chapter

Speed of change implies measurement – feedback on progress toward the vision and capabilities required to make strategy work. Most balanced scorecard efforts claim to do this, yet despite the hype, many companies have false starts and never get the benefit of the scorecard's promise to align everyone in the organization around a set of measures. In this chapter we lay out a step-by-step process to design and build a scorecard that measures up to the hype.

Performance measurement systems, or "balanced scorecards," are a key part of the overall business architecture and are closely linked to the corporate and business strategies. Given the business realities and change drivers at play, scorecards must do more than solely focus on past performance. Rather than looking in the rearview mirror, managers must learn how to read the road ahead. Stan Davis, author of *Future Perfect*, likens this to heat-seeking missiles that are capable of in-flight corrections to stay on track with the target ahead.

> Strategic control takes the tracking and checking-up characteristics of the control function, and rather than locating them in what has already happened, it places them in the future. It continually tracks how the future "X" is changing as you get closer to it, so that, although you are still managing to stated future objectives, the objectives are updated daily to correspond to the shifting reality.

Capable Companies not only know how to build capabilities and satisfy customers, they know how to track their progress. In other words, they get beyond the hype of the balanced scorecard and build strategic measurement and closed-loop feedback into their management system.

The Challenges

Getting the most from scorecards will continue to be elusive until business management strategy and data-management architecture are aligned. From a Capable Company perspective, we see the following challenges:

- Solving the scorecard conundrum: when and where to launch the effort.
- Aligning measures with the strategy.
- Taking an enterprise perspective.
- Driving accountability.
- Allowing performance measurements to be interdependent.

This chapter explores these challenges and provides tips for getting scorecard projects beyond PowerPoint slides to the information used to align and steer the organization.

Solving the Scorecard Conundrum: Where and When to Start

Companies are right to want measures that track strategy. Who wouldn't want a way to:

- emphasize and reinforce the company value-proposition;
- provide clear goals for accountability;
- track advantage capabilities;
- provide a clear logic path and line of sight from strategy to measures?

Leaders, however, are often perplexed as to why so-called balanced scorecards are often out of whack. The trouble usually starts from a false launch-point.

Many companies launch several concurrent scorecard projects and/or send multiple teams to scorecard workshops and conferences. Still many other companies sanction individual departments or groups to launch their own scorecards. While these initiatives appear to be positive steps or at least benign ones, they may very well cause problems.

Tip 1: The number of scorecards depends on the corporate strategy (see chapter 4)

- If you are an integrated company, that means you can't have different systems or different operational definitions of key measures. Start one project from the top.
  Caution: Although a corporate strategy implies a single business strategy, there is still the likelihood that if independent initiatives are launched from

various parts of the organization, the assumptions about strategy will likely be different.

- If you are an allied company, that means you have different business strategies for different companies. Launch a scorecard effort in one business unit, and then build on success.
  Caution: You'll want to leverage common systems and some common measures around shared customers and desired synergies.
- If you are a holding company, it is OK for different companies to pick their own scorecard system and have their own operational definitions for measures.
  Caution: Alignment problems can still occur in individual companies if different parts of that business have different assumptions about their business strategy.

Tip 2: Identify the business units and the best starting point.

Our experience has been that a scorecard launch succeeds best in a business unit that meets most of the following criteria:

- it has a strong operations champion
- it addresses real business challenge
- its customers have visibility to measures
- it has a strong continuous improvement program
- IT is part of the design team.

Aligning Measures with Business Strategy[1]

Once a team is commissioned to develop a scorecard, there are five keys to realigning measures to strategy:

1 Understanding the strategic implications of the Strategic Business Unit's (SBU's) "business focus" and "customer value proposition."
2 Mapping measures to capabilities.
3 Testing for fit.
4 Making a clear line of sight to the strategic measure.
5 Running a closed-loop system.

Business Strategy Implications

After spending an afternoon with his leadership team on scorecard design, a CEO protested: "these measures don't track our new strategy."

Business Focus	Customer Value Proposition				
	Low Cost	Quality	Speed	Service	Innovation
Product/ Service					
Customer/ Market					
Technology					
Production Capacity					
Distribution					

If there is consensus around distribution–speed, then key measures are …

Figure 9.1   Strategic Options Matrix

How does this happen?

All too often, measures are not cast in the context of the business strategy. As we recall from chapter 4, knowing the "Business Focus" choice and "Customer Value Proposition" should provide focus for capability development. It also suggests key measures.

For example, if a business focus is "distribution" and the customer value proposition is "speed," strategic measures would include on-time delivery, the gap between promised and shipping date, days late, etc.

If another company had a "product" business focus and a "quality" customer value proposition, strategic measures would include defects (e.g., part per million defective, yields, warranty costs, etc.).

A business focus of "technology" and customer value proposition of "innovation" would suggest new product measures such as time to market, revenue from new products, product derivatives, etc.

A business focus of "customer" and customer value proposition of "quality" would suggest key measures around CRM (see chapter 6): pipeline metrics on closing deals, fulfillment rates, and up-sell and cross-sell measures.

Tip 3: For each business unit identify 2–3 key measures based on business strategy (business focus and customer value proposition).

Map Measures to Capabilities

Another checkpoint to be sure you have strategic measures is to identify the key advantage capabilities and the process that delivers those capabilities. For example, the customer-interaction center company mentioned in chapter 1 had the advantage capabilities shown in table 9.1 driven by its businesses strategy (technology–service).

Table 9.1 Capabilities and Measures

Capability	Measure
Integrate the full spectrum of voice and Internet communications, including customer e-mail response, "chat," and extensive Web co-browsing capabilities	Technical functionality metrics
Deploy a sales development team that efficiently identifies potential clients with relevant needs	$ in opportunity pipeline
Provide B2B electronic channel and database management; help companies inform, acquire, service, grow, and retain their customers throughout the entire relationship life cycle	Service level agreement measures

Tip 4: Focus on advantage work (see chapter 4) then look for strategic measures for enabling processes. Focus on key cost/productivity measures when there is a significant performance gap in business necessity processes that should be at industry parity.

Capable Companies also link capabilities to the processes that deliver them and pull the results measures from those processes into the SBU scorecard (see the Enterprise View in figure 9.2). They also drive business process improvement through projects (see the Operations View in figure 9.2).

To accomplish this, companies need a business reporting architecture that ensures the right information is provided at the right time to match the decisions required.

At the enterprise level, operating and financial results are used to evaluate how functions and teams operate together to make strategy work. Financial reporting translates the operating data into summary data for top management. For example, as improvements in cycle time are made, this process information is passed up to the financial results as reduction in inventory and carrying costs. The data is needed monthly/quarterly to tell the story of how strategies have been executed.

At the process level, managers and teams need process targets (e.g., reduction of waste or cycle time, improvement in quality) and projects that act on

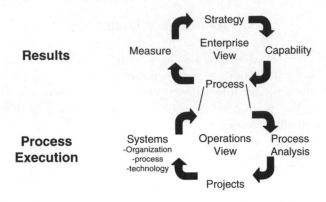

Figure 9.2   The Enterprise vs. the Operations View

the desired capabilities (e.g., guaranteed overnight delivery). These measures are timely, and close to the point of action. Feedback can be used to accurately adjust current projects and activities. This is the definition of a complete control loop.

In short, strategy determines the capabilities that are brought to life by business processes. Process measures allow them to be managed for optimal performance.

> **The beauty of developing strategic measures is that individuals and teams operating in the Operations View don't need to worry about the strategy but are aligned when capabilities are made clear.**

Test for Fit

To ensure alignment to strategy, both capabilities and measures must consider the operational archetype (see table 9.2).

In this example an inappropriate measure would be the number of decisions made by the first-line supervisor. This is the same reason why process benchmarking is often a red herring. Best practices can only be copied if the best-practice company has the same archetypes as your company. Capable

Table 9.2   Measures in Light of Archetype

Strategy	Management archetype	Capability	Measure
Global product launch	Command and control	Communicate up, across, and down	Decision cycle time

Companies worry more about building advantage capabilities that make it difficult for competitors to copy. They spend more time aligning measures to their business processes and operational archetypes and map those measures to the company's value and purpose.

Tip 5: Review the business architecture and archetypes and review the existing measures for fit.

Figure 9.3 shows the relationship between measures and archetypes.

The right side of figure 9.3 illustrates how a capability is influenced by the business archetype. For example, if you are a Holding Company, you need firewalls between businesses. This will have an impact on the capabilities of the company and how they share some technology and resources. On the left side of the figure, archetypes must be used to align incentives around the measure. For example, if the archetype for information access is closed (sometimes in a holding company), then it's inappropriate to encourage behaviors around sharing data. When establishing measures, archetypes are useful in providing guidelines to the most appropriate measures.

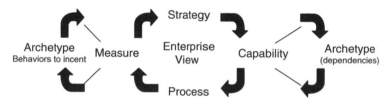

Figure 9.3   The Relationship Between Measures and Archetypes

Tip 6: Use a framework to identify gaps.

A framework such as the model in figure 9.4, developed by Results-Based Leadership, is useful in checking for omissions. However, we have encountered two problems in using this or other models:

Mistake 1   Assuming that balance means the same number of measures in each category. Balance refers more to the agenda for action. Are we solely focused on customer results at the expense of burning out our talent?

Mistake 2   Arguing whether something falls into one category or another. For example, is sales productivity an investor or employee measure? The right question is whether it is important in tracking strategy execution.

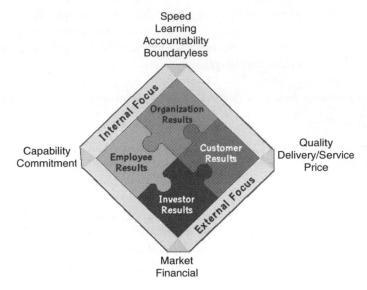

Figure 9.4   The Framework for a Balanced Scorecard

Clear Line of Sight

Leaders at each level are accountable for their measures since they own the resources and the process. As measures cascade down, they should be stated in the language of things, rather than financial terms (see figure 9.5).

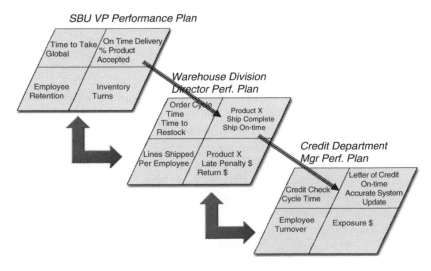

Figure 9.5   Line-of-Sight Metrics

It's not enough just to identify the measurement line of sight. Capable Companies use a planning process to assure that virtually every company action is aligned. For example, each year 3M's dental products division develops specific strategies, goals, and business plans during its annual strategic planning process. Once these goals are established, the company puts its business process management matrix to work by establishing teams and projects to accomplish objectives and identify measurement needs. Each project team is commissioned for the year to achieve a certain objective. This effort may include additions and revisions to the existing measures. 3M frequently reevaluates its scorecard to ensure that the measures are driving the right behaviors.[2]

Taking the Enterprise Perspective

Beyond the Analog Devices best practice, there are few enterprise-wide balanced scorecard implementations.[3] Yet this enterprise perspective lies at the heart of the concepts behind the balanced scorecard. To some extent, the development of enterprise resource-planning, Human Resources Information Systems (HRIS), and CRM systems will allow other companies to raise the balanced scorecard to the enterprise level.

Capable Companies recognize that they need both the systems and the data they provide, as well as a model such as one of those mentioned in this chapter, to provide true strategic insight. Getting the logic clear is a critical first step.

Caterpillar is one such company that has a fully integrated measurement system. The corporate office identifies the critical success factors that build strategies that shape the future. Bold goals are then developed by each of the profit centers in support of those critical success factors. Within the profit center each person and team has a set of smart goals. Smart goals are specific, measurable, achievable, results-oriented, and time bounded (SMART).[4]

A second step is required to prevent scorecard projects from ending up in PowerPoint decks rather than company guidance systems.

Tip 7: Be really clear about operational definitions and how they may change over time. Identify frequency, source, views, and access to data.

Teams need to remove ambiguity from their operational definitions. For example, the measure "on-time delivery" could be defined as "not late" or "not early and not late."[5] Companies also need to think about the reporting format: Should it be a table, line graph, or other? Based on the decisions being made, the frequency of the data needs to be examined. For example, on-time delivery needs to be reported on a monthly basis for operational improvement purposes, but perhaps daily or weekly from a customer status point of view. When developing scorecards the source of data is critical – are automated feeds available from the sales order system or CRM system? Finally, care must be taken as to how the data is to be viewed. What level of drill-down is helpful: by customer, by distributor, by product, etc.?

Paying attention of these issues transforms scorecards from intellectual curiosities into practical tools.

Driving Accountability

Perhaps the biggest challenge in building scorecards is to get leaders thinking beyond the measures themselves: setting goals, identifying and deploying responsibility, institutionalizing a good process improvement process, and forcing accountability at all levels.

According to Art Schneiderman, pioneer of the scorecard concept at Analog Devices:

> Many organizations stop measurement initiatives at setting priorities for stake-holders. Doing so leaves both the responsibility and accountability for improvement unassigned. They may achieve acceptance of the objective but leave undefined each individual's role in making it happen. Naturally, with this uncertainty, they usually conclude that closing critical performance gaps is someone else's job. Like spectators at an athletic event, they sit cheering in the stands, when they should in fact be out on the field as players in this struggle to win. The key to getting their involvement is the linkage of external improvement priorities to internal processes.

No Excuses: Getting and Delivering the Right Data

Managers often throw out a red herring: they use suspicion of data as an excuse for not fully deploying balanced scorecards. IT managers sometimes build systems to avoid data ownership issues. For example, IT can be a big help by providing:

- operational definitions of data (business logic)
- data edit and quality assurance rules
- definition of Systems of Record (schema logic)

- data-extraction and transformation rules
- data-aggregation rules
- data provisioning/loading
- flags on inconsistent data (reject files)
- the ability to audit data from an inquiry or report back to a system of record (drill-through).

Our experience suggests that:

1 Scorecard development is typically Business Necessity work and best outsourced, yet companies often try to build it themselves.
2 There are differences among different provider types (systems providers, e.g. Oracle or SAP; stand-alone scorecard providers, e.g., Pilot or CorVu; and business intelligence providers, e.g., Cognos or SAS) which must be factored into any decision, yet many companies assume the same features and functionality.

Allowing Performance Measurement to Be Interdependent

The timing of feedback loops discussed above is one sense of what the term "lead measure" means. In other words, report key operational data on a frequent basis, which allows the organization to respond quickly when measures are off-track. In this way corrective action can begin sooner rather than waiting for poor monthly or quarterly results.

Another aspect of *lead* and *lag* measures relates to the assumptions used in the scorecard model. Senior executives often expect instantaneous results in the financial or investor measures when they see an improvement in a customer or organization measure. Heated debates around this issue between operating managers and financial managers have been played out time and time again.

The root cause can be tied to the fact that external financial reporting and internal operational control represent two fundamentally different functions. The former is guided by Generally Accepted Accounting Practices (GAAP), tax laws, and the needs of stockholders, all lagging performance indicators. Operational control, on the other hand, is a leading performance indicator, and is guided by business strategy, and how well customer expectations are met. The lead–lag relationship comes down to a "trust-me" issue.

Art Schneiderman claims that there is not and cannot be a quantitative linkage between non-financial and expected financial results – but there is a soft link. Empirical research supports his claim. Several longitudinal studies verified the lead–lag relationship at a point in time. For example, companies that achieve fast cycle times later reported triple the revenue growth and double the profits over industry average competitors. However, given the many complex interactions between parts of an organization and its external environment, a quantified linkage is a stretch.

This logic illustrated in figure 9.6 used the Results-Based Leadership model.

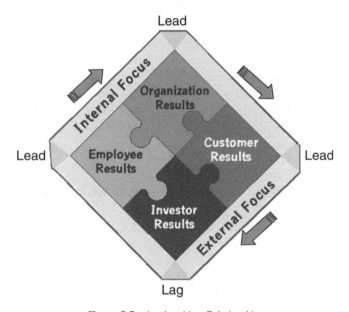

Figure 9.6 Lead and Lag Relationships

In the case of Analog Devices, the leadership team focused on attracting and retaining great designers (in new technologies such as digital signal processing), provided high visibility to new product volume and time to market, and paid attention to customer metrics *and* the quality system to continuously improve them. Over the years, these efforts have helped Analog improve production throughput rates (which delayed the need for adding capacity) and accelerated new product development – especially in the communications market (wireless applications and high-speed internet access).

The Building Blocks of the Capable Company

- Capable Companies tackle the scorecard conundrum head-on and make sure the scorecard initiative is aligned to their corporate strategy before they send groups off to get educated about scorecard practices.
- Capable Companies draw the relationship between strategy and capabilities, making it easier to draft measures that are truly strategic. They worry more about what is a good measure rather than in what bucket it belongs.
- Capable Companies not only know how to build capabilities and satisfy customers, they know how to track their progress. In other words, they get beyond the hype of the balanced scorecard and build measurements and closed-loop feedback into their management system.
- Capable Companies accept the hypothesis that employee, organization, and customer results will have a future impact on investor results. They also address the frequency of operational reporting so that they can raise a flag that a future result may not be reached unless corrective actions are taken.
- Capable Companies make the scorecard part of their planning process and integrate it with their leadership, customer, and process improvement processes.
- Capable Companies deal directly with the IT-related issues.
- Capable Companies use a scorecard as part of their management system. They:
    use the scorecard to set the operating committee agenda;
    link measures to quality improvement activities;
    link measures to competency models and rewards.
- Capable Companies know that Balanced Scorecard projects are predicated on the assumption that employee measures on commitment and competence will lead to desired organization capabilities such as new product time-to-market, which in turn lead to customer results in terms of quality, delivery, and price that impact the investor measures.
- Capable Companies recognize that lead measures are the independent variables that drive the investor or financial/market results. They view them as the collective wisdom of the organization about the indicators that will improve their odds of success.

Notes

1   See chapter 4.
2   *Measure What Matters: Aligning Performance Measures with Business Strategy* (APQC, 2000), p. 47.
3   Ibid.
4   Ibid., pp. 21–31.
5   In the late 1980s Analog Devices had been measuring on-time delivery. While the company was reporting 97 percent or better performance, a survey to customers revealed serious delivery problems. While the measure was the same, the operational definition important to the customer had changed from "not late" to "not late and not early" to meet new just-in-time (JIT) requirements of the customer. Analog corrected the definition and saw on-time delivery drop to 70 percent. It then focused process improvement teams to develop the capabilities to build and ship JIT.

10 Continually Refresh Capabilities

Even if you're on the right track, you'll get run over if you just sit there.

– Will Rogers

The Purpose of This Chapter

Returning to our gear metaphor, companies need tightly aligned strategy and change agendas. In this chapter, we provide the details of the process introduced in chapter 3. We cover the steps involved in sensing changes in the environment and aligning actions that respond to them. A case study is provided at the end of the chapter to illustrate a cycle of this process.

The Challenges

Capable Companies recognize that a top-down, command-and-control approach to change orchestration doesn't cut it. They must be able to sense threats and opportunities, then respond quickly and appropriately. Leaders must continually answer two questions: "Sense what?" and "Respond how?"

These questions beg for a process – a system that identifies the need for change and adjusts business capabilities accordingly.

A Model for Continual Business Alignment

An effective system will assure alignment among business capabilities and strategic objectives. A robust alignment process such as this will address:

- Sense
  - monitor the forces of change over time
  - identify those few Change Forces that must be addressed
  - identify the Business Capabilities that must be built, adapted, or shed

- Align
  - validate strategy choices
  - validate architectural choices
  - validate the current response and Business Capability agenda
- Respond
  - Adjust and communicate strategy and architectural choices
  - Create, augment, accelerate, or dismantle projects

A simple process is shown in figure 10.1 (begin at 9 o'clock and read anticlockwise). Pay rigorous attention to Change Forces in the environment to identify the subset that may cause change to the way that the company conducts business. These Change Drivers may influence the Organization, Process, or Technologies that enable Business Capabilities. When Business Capabilities change, Project Requirements must be set to create or alter Processes.

This process restates Strategy as the agenda of Business Capabilities. It is important to note that the model views Purpose, Mission, Vision, Values,

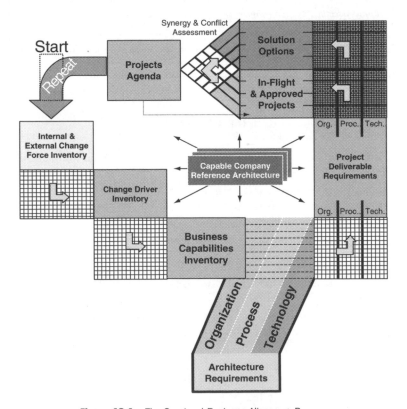

Figure 10.1   The Continual Business Alignment Process

and the Architectural choices (described in chapters 3, 7, and 8) as persistent Change Drivers. Such Drivers must be challenged frequently and adjusted accordingly to assure that they guide project design and, ultimately, capability solutions consistent with the desired business and organization outcomes.

In figure 10.1 connecting matrices represent a valuable audit trail, linking cause and effect for each change action.

Take Account of New Business Realities

The Continual Business Alignment tour starts with sensing for opportunities and threats (see figure 10.2).

Internal & External Change Force Inventory 	Change Forces:
	Those external and internal forces that are impacting the enterprise and may require it to move.
Change forces can be *external*, reflecting marketplace dynamics*:* • The Federal Reserve is expected to raise/cut interest rates by a half point. • A legal ruling is expected that may change the very fundamentals upon which the company was built (witness the break-up of AT&T, the anti-trust ruling against Microsoft, the "shut-down" of the Napster music file sharing service). • Competitors launch major advertising campaigns in key markets. • Moore's Law continues to unfold with micro-processor speed doubling roughly every 18 months. • The continuing expansion of broadband internet access to the home continues to reshape what is possible and economically viable with respect to internet-based service offerings.	**Change forces can be *internal*, reflecting strategic decisions, internal successes, failures or mandates:** • Leadership announces a change to the mission, vision or business strategy of the company (e.g. the company begins pursuing a strategy of growth through merger or acquisition). • A strategic decision is reached to enter new markets/launch a new business. • New executive team members will drive a new operating agenda. • A key technology implementation project is months behind schedule and well over budget. • A customer changes its process and places new requirements on its suppliers, such as raising quality expectations or having suppliers managing inventory.

Figure 10.2   Change Forces

Table 10.1 External Change Sources

External Sources	Description
Industry and Markets	Fundamental shifts in the marketplace are great sources of innovation and change.
Competitors	As competitors enter and exit the marketplace, change forces swirl. New threats and opportunities confront the company.
Customers	Very important and frequently overlooked sources of change forces are those people who purchase your product or service. They not only know you and your product but they also know your competitors. They will also create the future by demanding product features and services with which they are currently dissatisfied or which do not yet exist.
Technology	As the rate technological advancement quickens, so do the number of change forces.
Legal/Regulatory	Any entity that has the capacity to impose requirements upon the business must be viewed as a source for Change Forces. This not only applies to companies in highly regulated industries, but virtually all companies are impacted by laws to control energy usage, how employees can be treated, and safety in the workplace.

The first step in "Sensing" is the structured monitoring of what is happening outside and what is changing within the environment. The sensing nodes found in tables 10.1 and 10.2 can be used to capture Change Forces.

As can be seen from table 10.3, change events have diverse characteristics.

Forces may be revealed from many venues, including feedback collected from customers, suppliers, employees, and investors; from sales or service calls, or from customer complaints; from individual interviews or focus groups. Here are sample interview questions used to reveal Change Forces:

- *What industry trends have been influencing/impacting your company?*
- *What competitive issues are you dealing with in your business unit?*
- *What must your business unit do to contribute to the company's success?*
- *What is bogging down your operations?*
- *Areas for exploration:*
    Customer requirements
    Meeting customer expectations
    Supplier issues
    Product design/manufacturability issues
- *What cultural changes are needed to meet the present and future needs of the business?*

Table 10.2 Internal Change Sources

Internal Sources	Description
Corporate Strategy	Any shift in model (e.g., a holding company transforming to an allied model will see an explosion in capability requirements surrounding the integration and leveraging of shared services).
Business Strategy	A shift in business focus or customer value proposition.
Company Leaders and Subject-Matter Experts	Knowledgeable persons in various functions and at various levels of the company are primary sources for change forces. Either because of their leadership position or their recognized expertise within the company, these people have knowledge of how the industry is changing. They also frequently have "tribal knowledge" about how the organization has evolved. Interviews with these people, focusing on "What's changing in and around the company?" and "How must the company change and why?" will reveal many forces.
Measurement Systems	As with many dashboards and scorecards, it is usually when a measure deviates outside of a control limit that management attention is flagged and it becomes a change force.

Table 10.3 Source of Change

Types of Events	Characteristics	Example
Cyclical	These are changes that repeat over time in an established and routine pattern.	• The "El Niño" weather pattern. • Annual events such as Christmas.
Predictable	The occurrence is fairly certain, but the exact timing is far less certain.	• The flooding of the Mississippi. • Demographic shifts.
Trends	Really a series of events that are less significant ... you need to pick one of those places where you'll let it impact you.	• Changes in fashion. • The political influence of the US Latino population.
Unpredictable	Events that impact businesses which they could not realistically have foreseen.	• Scientific discovery. • The outbreak of a war.

A hefty amount of data can be accumulated from the Change Force identification process. Much of this data is qualitative data, and as with any "voice-of-the-customer" exercise, care should be taken to make statements clear and unambiguous.[1]

All change forces are not to be addressed equally. Factual Change Forces (e.g., "Our largest customer just went bankrupt") must be separated from those that are anticipated (e.g., "We anticipate triple-digit growth in our widgets business next year"). For those that are anticipated, probability of occurrence will help to set weighing factors, as will consideration of time frames. Table 10.4 offers an example of how a Change Force Inventory may be constructed.

Table 10.4   Change Force Inventory Template

Change Force	Fact or Projection	Probability of Occurrence	Degree of Confidence	Projected Time Frame
Supplier X has filed for bankruptcy	Fact	100%	100%	Now
Price of critical widget component to increase by 50%	Projection	75%	High	6–9 months

Documentation and maintenance of a Change Force Inventory prevents the need to build this list from scratch each time an alignment assessment is conducted. Some forces demand a heightened sense of awareness... these go on a watch list that is monitored with high frequency. The Internet was one such force. Most companies knew it was growing and evolving and that it might cause them to change (both on a grand scale and quickly), so they monitored it closely.

Additional high-awareness forces might include competitors entering the market, competitor market-share numbers, the financial stability of suppliers, behavior shifts, or generational/demographic shifts within target markets. Future assessments and discussions with leaders can begin with the existing inventory and the questions: "What has changed?" and "What else should we be watching?"

Extract Change Drivers

Hundreds of Change Forces can be resolved to a critical subset that demands attention. Those that individually or collectively drive change to the way in which it conducts business are Change Drivers (see figure 10.3). In many cases, a force may be present for some time without generating a Change Driver but when several forces converge (as in the music industry example below), a Change Driver becomes apparent. Because Change Drivers demand changes to the Business Capability Inventory, they serve as the catalyst for change.

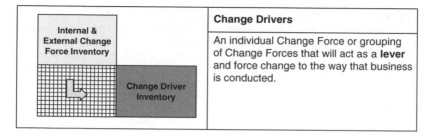

Figure 10.3 Change Drivers

The following example for the music recording industry shows how a number of individual Change Forces did not pose a threat to the recording industry, but collectively, they formed a very clear and compelling Change Driver.

Change Forces:
Technology has enabled the local storage and duplication of digital music

- significant advances in digital compression technology for audio (MP3)
- continued growth in the hard-disk storage space of PCs
- CD burners for PCs and blank media have continually become more affordable
- "ripping" software enables extraction of copyrighted music to hard disk

Technology has enabled the interconnectivity of an unlimited number of people sharing an unlimited number of files

- continued rapid growth of the number of households with Internet access
- continued growth in Internet bandwidth
- membership of file-sharing services, such as Napster, experiencing significant monthly growth.

Change Driver:
Millions of copyrighted music files are being "downloaded" for free over the Internet and burned to personal CDs, bypassing the traditional music distribution network.

Table 10.5 shows how a Change Driver Inventory is constructed. In addition, Change Forces that drive the creation of Change Drivers are also linked to produce an audit trail and accelerate future cycles (not shown). Companies may also consider what they can do to increase their degree of confidence in their predictions, such as purchasing market research or enlisting help from

Table 10.5   Change Driver Inventory Template

Change Driver	Strategic Impact	Probability of Impact	Projected Time Frame	Shifts/ Trends	Possible Response(s)
Millions of copyrighted music files are being "downloaded" for free over the Internet and burned to personal CDs, bypassing the traditional music distribution network	Millions of dollars in lost revenue	100%	Now	Number of monthly downloads and number of file-sharing utilities projected to continue to grow	• Legal action • Encryption research • Launch own on-line distribution • Revise business model to leverage artists' live performances

experts. In addition, they can consider what they can do to influence the probability of a desired outcome, such as lobbying favorable legislation or hiring a key player away from a competitor.

Identify Business Capabilities

Business capabilities build a bridge between "Sense" and "Respond." They are actionable in the form of processes and projects. Whereas Change Drivers establish "why" a capability must be created or changed, Business Capabilities establish "what" must happen (see figure 10.4).

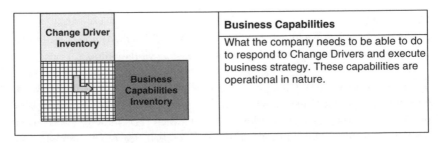

Figure 10.4   Business Capabilities

Table 10.6 Identifying Business Capabilities

Change Forces	Change Driver	Business Capability
Customers demand to use multiple communications channels, including face-to-face, mail, telephone, Web, videoconference, e-mail, fax, interchangeably and seamlessly	Transform "call centers" into "customer-interaction centers" through skill development, education, and IT	Continuously redefine the state of the art in customer-interaction technology, systems, integration capabilities, and operations
		Manage the transition of capabilities into operations through training and performance management
	Integrate data so that all conversations (before and during care), regardless of medium or point of interaction, will be accessible at all other points of interaction and through all customer-interaction media	Integrate customer interaction-system data (including relevant interaction history) with client-systems data
		Provide conversion of data among customer-interaction platforms

The example in table 10.6 for a "customer-care company" illustrates relationships among Change Forces, Change Drivers and Business Capabilities. Typically, application of this method will yield 25–40 drivers and capabilities. In actuality, the relationship between these elements is many-to-many, since a Change Driver can exist in response to multiple change forces. The same holds for the relationship between drivers and capabilities (e.g., building an automated 24-hour telephone self-service capability can be in response to a Change Driver: "improving customer satisfaction with automated support" as well as "reducing operational costs").

Business Capabilities facilitate the transformation of strategy to action by providing a clear set of requirements to all line and staff functions that can be planned for, acted upon, and delivered. Projects will ultimately establish "how" the company will deliver or adjust Business Capabilities.

Before setting an agenda to adjust Business Capabilities, a forward look helps to avoid knee-jerk reactions with negative consequences. After applying the method described in chapter 5 to categorize capabilities into those that provide competitive advantage from those that are merely necessary, consideration of their future value and performance levels will help guide action. Some capabilities will need to be created; some will need to be modified; the performance level of some capabilities may be overkill, while others may fall short. Table 10.7 suggests several possible transformations.

Table 10.7 Capabilities Transformation

Transformation Type	Description	Change Capability Performance By:
Create/Acquire	Non-existence to full-blown capability realization	0 to X
Reinvent	Completely change the manner in which the capability is realized	X to X via a new means.
Radical Improvement	Major capability changes to realize 10X improvement in a key capability measure	X to 10X
Incremental Improvement	Minor capability changes to realize a noticeable improvement in a key capability measure	X to X + 10%
Outsource	Business Necessity work or strategic support work where the gap is too large	Outsourcing project with service level agreements
Steady State	Maintain capability performance at current levels	X to X
Acceptable Decline	The capability, while necessary, is performing beyond levels dictated by strategy. A decline is acceptable to yield savings (e.g., an Advantage Capability becomes a Business Necessity Capability)	X to X − 10%
Drop/Disable	The capability is no longer necessary, as dictated by strategy. The capability is disabled and removed from the process portfolio	X to 0

A completed inventory (table 10.8) will likely have 25–75 Business Capabilities that reflect strategic intent.

Updating Architecture Requirements

In chapter 7, we introduced architecture as a set of references that Capable Companies use as they build capabilities. Architecture Requirements (shown

Table 10.8   Business Capability Inventory

Business Capability	Type of Work Current/ (Prior)	Performance Gap	Trans- formation Required	Time Frame for Capability Realization
Provide nationwide next- day delivery for product orders received late in the evening	Advantage/ Strategic Support	Current: next-day delivery for orders placed before 4 P.M. EST Target: next-day delivery for orders placed before 10 P.M. EST	Reinvention or radical improvement	2–4 months

in figure 10.5) guide the way in which people work; processes are designed, measured, and managed; and infrastructure is built; and the deployment of processes and the organization and technology that enable them.

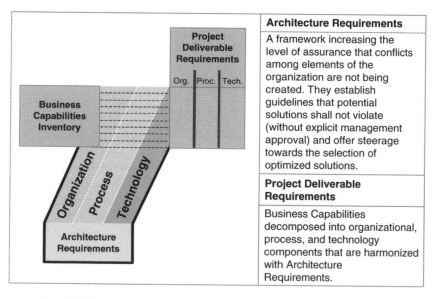

Figure 10.5   Architecture Requirements and Project-Deliverable Requirements

Given that there are many ways of creating a capability, Architecture Requirements establish a degree of appropriateness or fit. For example: the two banks shown in table 10.9 deliver " banking services" to customers, but given that they are driven by differing Business Focus and Customer Value Propositions, Architectural implications are considerable. Capability enabling solutions must consider these carefully.

Table 10.9 Comparison of Architectural Implications

Business Focus/Value Prop.	Bank 1 Distribution/Price	Bank 2 Customer – Market/Service
Organization Architecture Implications	Size, standards, and the resultant economies of scale drive profitability. "Command and control" keeps the machine working. Individualism within the culture will likely be a liability.	Customer intimacy drives success. Decision making is distributed so that it takes place close to the customer. Command and control would probably fail. Individualism within the culture can be an asset.
Process Architecture Implications	Again, driven by standards and the resultant economies of scale, processes are rigid.	Driven by a desire to foster a customer-oriented environment, there is a high degree of flexibility built into processes. Inflexible processes are likely to fail.
Technology Architecture Implications	Mergers, acquisitions, and divestitures drive the expansion and optimization of the distribution network. An integrated technology platform would slow acquisitions and prevent divestitures.	Bringing data and associated services to the customer interface becomes key. An integrated technical architecture assists the attainment of this goal.

Over time, Architecture Requirements must be adaptable. Take the example of a manufacturer whose growth had been driven by acquisition and its success by business-unit autonomy. The company was a de-facto holding company. When the company examined its Change Drivers (see table 10.6), it saw that its desire for higher operating margins was hampered by redundant Business-Necessity capabilities in all of the operating units. It also saw that growth was hampered by the inability of product development teams and marketing teams to effectively share information. These drivers made it readily apparent to the management team that the holding-company archetype that had supported operational autonomy was no longer valid.

The company was in a state of transition from a "holding company" to an "allied company." To manifest its new spirit of collaboration, the company launched an extensive cross-company intranet initiative to consolidate Business Necessity human resources processes and foster cross-divisional processes to leverage information sharing in product development and marketing.

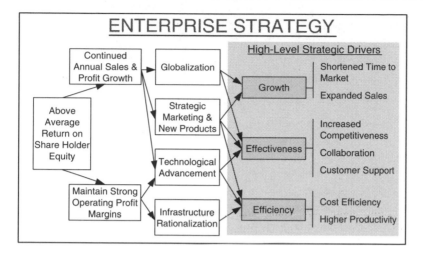

Figure 10.6   Enterprise Strategy

Tuning Capabilities Through Projects

The work to capture Change Forces, identify Change Drivers, define Business Capabilities, and test against Architecture Requirements delivers a clear view of "what" must be delivered to the enterprise. Project creation and/or modification will finally establish "how" capabilities will be deployed (see figure 10.7).

The current portfolio of projects serves as a jumping-off point for adjustment of Business Capabilities. As potential solutions are considered and begin to take shape in the form of project proposals, they need to be considered in a holistic context, examining capability gaps, need and implementation time frames, and considering synergies and conflicts with all other proposals and projects.

A software development company utilized this process and built a Projects/Capabilities Matrix (see table 10.10) to assess how and if the frenetic level of

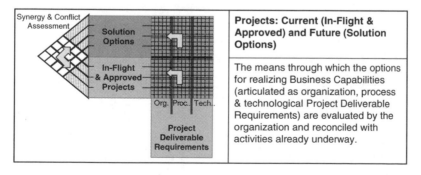

Figure 10.7   Current and Future Projects

Table 10.10 Projects/Capabilities Matrix (Partial)

Priority→	1	2	3	4	5	6
Top Business Capability needs as determined by executive management →	Effective means for prospects to understand the company: - Image, Brand, Product, Value Prop., Product Appl., Product Tech.	Provide a clear statement of Purpose, Mission, Values, Vision, Strategy & goals so that it is meaningful to each employee.	Establish our company as a branded thought leader in our application space	Continually increase the value of Human Assets through coaching, training, experience and challenge.	Apply the right people to the most valuable work at the right time.	Build Vertical Applications collaboratively with experts and re-use, re-purpose & continually improve them.
Business Capability Type →	**Adv. Cap.**	**Strat. Supt.**	**Adv. Cap.**	**Strat. Supt.**	**Adv. Cap.**	**Adv. Cap.**
In-Flight & Planned Projects						
Redesign the Internet Site						
Redesign Technical Capabilities						
Engineer the Internet portal	H		L			H
Support Streaming Video	M		M			
Verify Security Capabilities	H		L			H
Support VPN Through the Firewall	H		L			H
Instrument and Report Usage	H					
Provide Secure FTP						H
Redesign Look & Feel	M		H			H
Add Content						
Investor Relations	M		M			

Redesign the Intranet Site

Instrument and Report Usage	L	
Add Content	M	M
Content Project 1 (Revamp the portal)		
Content Project 2 (TBD)	L	

Stabilize Personal Computing

Set PC Platform Standards
Set Workgroup Server Standard
Set Workgroup Server Software Std

activity within the company was truly contributing to strategic goals. Over fifty business capabilities were identified and prioritized, the top six of which are provided in the matrix. (Note: This team bypassed Project Deliverable Requirements and mapped projects directly to capabilities.)

The team identified all projects that were currently in flight or well into the planning stage. Examining intersection points between these two inventories and assessing the degree (High/Medium/Low/None) to which each project, as presently constructed, contributed to desired Business Capabilities revealed opportunities for adjustment of the project agenda:

- Many projects that were contributing to the realization of the same capability turned out to be task-focused projects operating in ignorance of the needed Business Capability and/or the agendas of other projects targeting the realization of that same capability.
- There were Advantage Capabilities that did not have any projects associated with them at the high or medium correlation level.
- There were many projects that contributed to the realization of only Business Necessity or non-essential capabilities.

With this insight in hand, the team was able to begin the process of rethinking their efforts, with a focus on the delivery of Advantage and Strategic Support Capabilities. Tools such as this help formulate and prioritize projects by clearly relating current and planned project work to all Business Capabilities, Types of Work, and capability performance goals. For example:

- there may be a missing Advantage Capability that has no project activity; or
- a Business Necessity Capability may have several active projects focused on taking that capability to performance levels not required by the strategy; or
- projects whose deliverables are required on a longer time frame are receiving more attention than projects with more timely demand; or
- projects that have an attractive return on investment but do not deliver strategically important capabilities; these will drain critical resources and management attention from projects with greater potential.

With this insight, new projects can be proposed and current efforts can be reconstituted.

Changing the Course of In-Flight Projects

In most companies, once a project is launched the focus shifts from Justification to Completion. This is particularly true with major IT initiatives. Once a project is launched with the expressed purpose of delivering a specific Business Capability, management can continually gauge the business's need for the capability, and reflect this through the project's goals, resources, and support. When Change Drivers impact the relative importance of capabilities being delivered by a project, management is left with a handful of options (see table 10.11).

Table 10.11   Project Redirection Options

Project Option	Context
Do nothing	Project deliverables evaluated at the time of project approval and financial ROI, are still reasonable – plow forward based upon the project's original underlying assumptions.
Accelerate the project	The capability is more important than before – remove obstacles, implement a rapid decision-making process to give projects adequate guidance, empower project managers to secure appropriate resources, provide appropriate incentives to project teams, etc.
Decelerate the project	The need for the capability is less certain than before – consider revisiting the timetable based on new information or possibly outsource the activity.
Re-mission the project	The capability requirements have changed – build on data collected and analyzed but change the performance goals and measures that may impact the solution.
Shut down the project	The capability is no longer strategic – it is both in the best interests of the company, as well as the project team, to shut down the project. Eliminating some projects frees up scarce resources to work on the projects that have higher value contribution to strategy.

Orchestrating a Projects Agenda

Having established clearly prioritized Business Capabilities, and clarified to the best of its ability the context of its present and anticipated future environment, a company is in a position to prepare for action by developing a Projects Agenda (see figure 10.8).

Projects may be launched to build new capabilities, improve existing capabilities, or dismantle and eliminate them. When management prioritizes the

Business Capabilities List, it provides an instrument panel to guide resource allocation and course correction for in-flight projects.

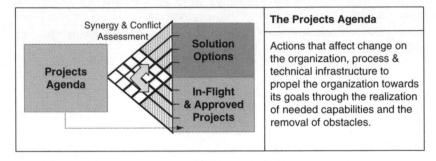

Figure 10.8   The Projects Agenda

Table 10.12 gives a short list of considerations when scoping a project.

Table 10.12   Considerations When Scoping a Project

Project description	• What problem is being solved?
	• What capabilities does it deliver?
	• How will it be measured? What capability gap will be closed?
	• What is the pattern of investments?
	• What are the downstream decision points?
	• Are there interdependencies with other projects?
Risk	• What is the amount of risk that must be borne to create value?
	• Can the risk be shared with partners or customers?
	• Does the company have past experience with similar projects?
Volatility	• What are the sources of uncertainty that make flexibility valuable?
	• Are there foreseeable/predictable changes?
Value to cost	• What is the business payoff?
	• Are there predictable losses associated with deferring investments?
	• Is there value in breaking up projects?
	• What downstream investment might be required?

Effective management of the Business Capability agenda involves engaging executives in the evaluation of *which* projects should be funded and *when*. Figure 10.9 provides a means of visualizing the complex juxtaposition of project value, risk, and potential timing implications. Questions such as the following must be considered:

- Which projects are appropriate to launch at this time?
- Which projects are candidates for launch if changes to risk or value occur?
- Which projects should clearly be reconstituted or taken off the board?

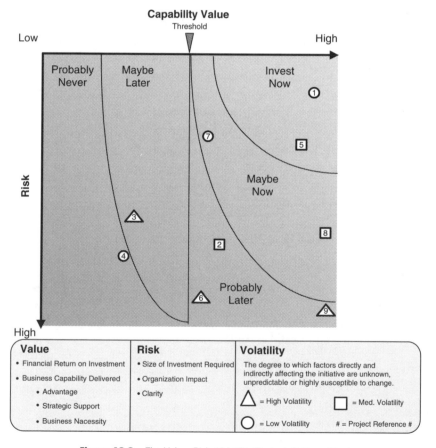

Figure 10.9   The Value, Risk, Volatility/Project Options Chart

A balanced portfolio first focuses on high-value projects that deliver Advantage Capabilities. A careful assessment of risk, return, and volatility drives the remainder of the project agenda.

Coming Full Circle

In addition to generating several new internal change forces, the Intranet project presented above required the company to rethink some architectural requirements pertaining to its people-management systems. Prior to the Intranet, the three CIOs of the major business units each enjoyed complete autonomy. The Intranet initiative changed that, creating with its deployment new architectural requirements, both for collaboration and for the need to assess new initiatives for cross-functional impact. This highlights how the continual alignment process comes full circle and how events and decisions made during a single iteration become forces of change in the next.

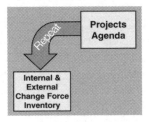

Figure 10.10   Continually Reassess the Agenda

Table 10.13 shows how all of the elements of a continual business-alignment cycle interconnect. (The case study "Example of a Capability Refresh Cycle," at the end of this chapter, provides a data-level example and illustrates the power of building and adapting capabilities.)

Table 10.13 From Change Forces to Projects

Change Forces	Those external and internal forces that are impacting the enterprise and may require it to move.
Reveal critical ...	
Change Drivers	An individual compelling Change Force or grouping of Change Forces that will act as a **lever** upon the company and force it to alter the way it does business.
Which must be responded to with...	
Business Capabilities	What the company needs to be able to do to execute its business strategy (e.g., support customers through any medium – phone, web, etc.). These capabilities are operational in nature.
Which place unique demands and dynamics on the company's...	
Organizational, Process, & Technological infrastructure	Those people, process, and technology "systems" that interact with one another to get work done. These become Project Deliverable Requirements.
Which must function within parameters set by...	
Architectural Requirements	A framework within which the company can act on the delivery of capabilities, thereby greatly increasing the level of assurance that conflicts with other elements of the organization are not being created. They establish guidelines that potential solutions may not violate (without explicit management approval) and offer steerage toward the selection of an optimal solution.
That are realized through...	
Projects	Actions that affect change on the organization, process, & technological infrastructure to propel the organization towards its goals through the realization of needed capabilities and the removal of obstacles.

The Building Blocks of the Capable Company

Companies that are disciplined take the time to scan the environment, distill change drivers, understand their impact on capabilities, and move quickly to appropriate action. They also periodically refresh their architecture to assure alignment and enablement. Their Projects Agenda is laser-focused and routinely reviewed for alignment with desired results:

Continued

- Capable Companies are very good at sorting through the "noise" and accurately identifying internal and external change "influences" that will cause the company to change.
- Capable Companies are "built to change" and can "turn on a dime" because they have capable leaders and have deployed processes and infrastructure with a focus on agility.
- Capable Companies know *why* they're doing what they're doing.
- Capable Companies know the value of all the Business Capabilities being delivered so they can intelligently repurpose resources in the face of change.
- Capable Companies recognize that the Organization Capabilities (talent, speed, collaboration, learning, accountability) are not the "soft stuff." They are the differentiating factors in winners and losers and can be codified in the company's organization architecture.
- Capable Companies make certain that all employees, no matter what level of the organization, are working toward the delivery of the same set of capabilities.
- Capable Companies adjust the course of projects, changing the capabilities that the projects deliver.
- Capable Companies continually evaluate the impact that changes to the Mission/Vision/Purpose have on their Business Architecture choices.
- Capable Companies continually empower and unify their employees by focusing on results (Capabilities), not means (Project requirements stated as features and functions).
- Capable Companies make certain that the skills and attributes of all employees, including and especially leaders, are adaptable to realize and sustain the changing capability requirements of the business.

Note

1   In our experience, companies often struggle to understand qualitative data. Some understanding of semantics – the study of words and meaning and how people communicate – is critical at this stage of analysis. Just as an engineer watches out for data that is skewed or biased, teams need to be on guard for possibilities in misinterpreting the language data collected. In processing language data (i.e., converting information for company use), customer voices are often distorted or

masked. What customers say can be mixed with affection, abstraction, inference, judgment, or two-valued thinking (a two-valued orientation considers information to exist in one of two states, e.g., good or bad, fast or slow, easy or hard). For customer requirements to be understood, they need to be stated in clear, measurable terms.

CASE STUDY: EXAMPLE OF A CAPABILITY REFRESH CYCLE

Inside a Retail Chain Startup

The following example highlights how a retail chain startup responded to convert an initial investment in four retail stores from a 10 percent per quarter investment rate to 20 percent per quarter profit through self-financed expansion, in eight quarters.

The Challenge

Design the company's infrastructure components to fit cash-flow constraints, future cost models, and the corporate culture.

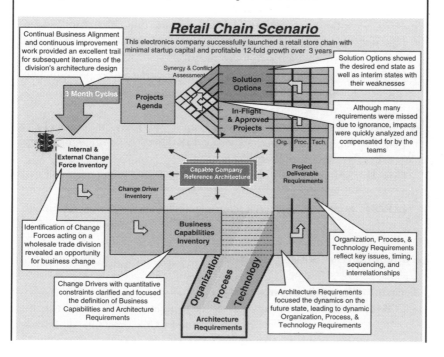

Continued

Change forces [CF]

[CF-1] Restocked finished goods are building up and future returns are projected to exceed the capacity of current outlet channels.

[CF-2] Retail channel growth is at a plateau and is projected to remain flat.

[CF-3] A major customer is expected to become a manufacturer/ competitor.

[CF-4] Wholesale channel margins are becoming dangerously slim.

[CF-5] Factory outlet complexes are prospering across the country.

Change drivers [CD]

[CD-1] Develop a chain of retail outlets for restocked goods in accordance with wholesale channel sales performance and financial constraints.

[CD-2] Ensure profitability to offset wholesale channel margin shrinkage.

Capabilities [C]

[C-1] Process, technology, and organization infrastructure to support development and operation of a chain of 25 factory-outlet stores within 2 years and more than 50 within 3 years.

[C-2] Management structure to support a distributed workforce and relatively high employee turnover.

[C-3] Rapid and effective means of training store personnel in product capabilities, differentiation, and demonstration.

Architectural requirements [AR]

[AR-1] Support multiple, short-cycle iterations of business processes at the head office and in stores.

[AR-2] Introduce scalable head-office systems to support explosive growth.

[AR-3] Support a half-week planning and replenishment cycle time to minimize committed inventory and maximize flexibility.

Project deliverable requirements

Technology requirements [TR]

[TR-1] Leverage existing systems to expedite startup, minimize investment, and delay commitment to infrastructure until business processes are stable.

[TR-2]   Design and deploy in-store and home-office systems that minimize cash flow in the early stages when investment capital is scarce and risk is high.

[TR-3]   Introduce scalable systems to support a 25-store chain spread over 20 of the contiguous 48 states within 12 months, and 50 stores, with Hawaii added, in the following year.

Organization requirements [OR]

[OR-1]   Retail business compensation.

[OR-2]   Highly dispersed/small-operation communications.

[OR-3]   Retail operation security, privacy, and trust.

Process requirements [PR]

[PR-1]   Retail personnel, recruiting, and training processes.

[PR-2]   Simultaneous deployment of a 4-store network and the design of a 25-store network.

[PR-3]   Small customer (store) replenishment from main warehouse.

[PR-4]   Tailored forecasting to include restocked goods planning.

Results

Employing an architectural design for the retail chain's system of people, process, and technology, the teams quickly identified essential components, created them, and qualified them. Knowing what subsequent iterations would look like allowed simultaneous deployment and validation of iteration one while designing and qualifying components for iteration two. Convergence on acceptable solutions in all three dimensions (organization, process, and technology) was rapid, and convergence on optimized solutions was smooth:

- Capital availability drove speed and thrift to allow early store profits to fund later store openings. Realizing this early in the game forced the teams to focus on essential processes and capabilities.
- Knowing that the initial support systems could not be scaled forced an iterative approach to design, deployment, and improvement.
- A shared understanding of system weaknesses encouraged tolerance and cross-functional support.
- A shared understanding of the issues encouraged risk taking.

Epilogue:
Governance in a Capable Company

Capable companies move swiftly and purposefully, but this is only an external view. What is not seen from the outside is the thoughtful application of experience, evolution, experimentation, and failure that propels them. Every company mentioned in this book is a strong competitor and a high performer not because it was faster or smarter, but rather because each was both fast *and* smart. At the same time, no two of the companies shared more than a few strengths. Therein lies their potential to be even more capable in the future.

The Governance of Capabilities

This book is all about capabilities: choosing those that are necessary, building them, tuning them to strategy, deploying them, and synchronizing the interdependency of Organization and Business Capabilities that create value for employees, customers, investors, and the organization itself. In many companies the gears fail to mesh owing to a lack of explicit management attention.

It is the job of every leader to build and maintain value-adding capabilities. However, in lean organizations, where leaders have broad spans of control, their attention gravitates to getting the work done at superior levels of quality and continually reducing costs. Even at the highest levels of leadership, attention is frequently drawn away from infrastructure issues and focused outward to investors and customers.

Leaders of Capable Companies put capability building at the top of their other number-one priorities, and the most progressive ones do so formally. They institutionalize governance practices in order to sharpen focus on strategy, align the anchor points that build culture, and maintain a unique way of working that competitors can't copy. They architect, measure, and manage their business processes and enable them with competent and committed people; they enable their people with adaptable technology; and they relentlessly manage the profitability of their products and customer relationships.

Shifting the Governance Gears

When companies stray from executing their strategy to make quarterly numbers, chase a pot of gold, or react without thinking, they lose momentum. They need to downshift the gears, burn excessive energy, and come back up to speed. When this happens frequently, they learn to operate in the wrong gear most of the time, shifting constantly and building an activity culture rather than a performance culture.

Some companies err in the opposite direction by setting annual goals and sticking to some of them and not to others, thereby confusing, if not disenfranchising, employees. This is analogous to driving in high gear all the time. The company does not slow down quickly, but it can't accelerate quickly either, resulting in a "wait-and-see" culture.

Active governance of capabilities ensures that the right gears are in place and that the right gear is in use most of the time. Purpose, Mission, Values, Culture, Vision, Strategy, Capabilities, Processes, and Competencies may all change over time as companies sense their environment and respond to it. Governance assures that a required change to any of these cogs does not interfere with the others. Such a requirement makes annual planning cycles obsolete for all but a few companies.

Governance Simplified

Archetypes simplify capability design by allowing the combination of a few choices to eliminate many capability options from consideration. The application of tools simplifies selection and tuning capabilities to strategy. Building basic Organization Capabilities and a strong leadership team provides organizations with agility. What remains is rigor and method.

Rigor comes from executive attention to capability building and performance management. It is enhanced by the frequent assessment of goals and the ability of current and future Organization and Business Capabilities to achieve those goals. As frequently as possible, the executive team should have thoughtful answers to the question: "Will we have the capability to reach our goals and, if not, which capabilities need to be adjusted, and who is accountable for doing this?"

A governance process that imposes little administrative overhead, enables the rapid execution of short cycles, and aligns line and staff functions in a single pass complements the model of the Capable Company.

The Past and the Future

Many paths led to the content of this book, including Leadership Development, Quality of Management, Total Quality Management, Six Sigma, Work-Out, Lean Management, Rapid Product Design, Customer Relationship Management, Strategy Planning, Change Management, and Business Process Engineering. Independently, each path has proven valuable and aligned application of several of them has proven even more valuable.

As we followed these paths, it became obvious that it is the journey that institutionalizes capabilities within organizations and that acquired capabilities propel organizations forward. Generalizing the idea to include all business and organization capabilities revealed the "second language" for describing strategy. In effect, creating a Rosetta Stone that translates strategy to aligned action.

Companies are focused on results as always but they are turning attention to their organizations' ability to sustain investor, customer, and employee confidence to a more distant horizon. Back to our roots, tuning our culture, fiscal responsibility, core competencies, and other introspective pursuits will benefit from sharp focus on "capability building" as the pathway for the journey to The Capable Company.

Suggested Reading

Leadership

How Leaders Build Market Value – David Ulrich and Norm Smallwood (Wiley, 2003). How leaders build value and trust.

Results Based Leadership – David Ulrich, Jack Zenger, and Norm Smallwood (Harvard Business School Press, 1999). A landmark book, *Results-Based Leadership* challenges the conventional wisdom surrounding leadership. The authors argue that it is not enough to gauge leaders by personal traits such as character, style, and values. Rather, effective leaders know how to connect their leadership attributes with results.

On Becoming a Leader, Warren Bennis (Addison Wesley, 1994). In this classic leadership guide, Bennis identifies the key ingredients of leadership success and offers a game plan for cultivating those qualities.

Leading Change, John P. Kotter (Harvard Business School Press, 1996). Kotter's thesis is that strategies for change often fail in corporations because the changes do not alter behavior. He identifies the most common mistakes in effecting change, offering eight steps to overcoming obstacles.

Managerial Breakthrough: A New Concept of the Manager's Job, Joseph M. Juran (McGraw Hill, 1964). Excellent book on reactive problem solving and organization change management.

The 48 Laws of Power, Robert Greene and Joost Elffers (Viking, 1998). A compilation of many authors on the use and abuse of power, however it is acquired.

Leadership and the New Science, Margaret J. Wheatly (Berret-Koehler, 1992). A thoroughly readable yet scientific treatise of organizations and organic systems.

Changing the Essence: The Art of Creating and Leading Fundamental Change in Organizations, Richard Beckhard and Wendy Pritchard (Jossey-Bass, 1992). A clear and concise statement of why change must affect the essence of an organization to take hold and yield results.

Strategy

Creating the Corporate Future: Plan or be Planned For, Russell L. Ackoff (John Wiley & Sons, 1981). Ackoff talks about "interactive management" and planning backwards.

Innovation & Entrepreneurship: Practice & Principles, Peter F. Drucker (HarperCollins, 1986). Based on Drucker's research in the 1950s to 1970s, this book unlocks the mystery of innovation. Written in 1980 but still timely.

Northbound Train, Karl Albrecht (American Management Association, 1994). Albrecht presents a process for formulating a vision and a direction for a company and communicating that vision in a compelling way to everyone in the organization.

Real-Time Strategy, W. Norman Smallwood, Lee Tom Perry, and Randall G. Scott (Wiley, 1993). The authors stress the importance of implementing "real-time" strategies, which are performed on the job and handled by people throughout the company – right down to the operating level.

Business Alignment

A New American TQM, Shoji Shiba, Alan Graham, and David Walden (Productivity Press, 1993). This is Shiba's compilation of the work he did with the Center for Quality Management (CQM) in Cambridge, Massachusetts.

Process Innovation: Reengineering Work Through Information Technology, Thomas Davenport (Harvard Business School Press, 1992). Good ideas about the role of information technology in organization/process design.

E-Business and ERP: Transforming the Enterprise, Grant Norris et al. (Wiley, 2000). Good insight to the impact of ERP on people, process, and technology.

Organizing Genius: The Secrets of Creative Collaboration, Warren Bennis and Patricia Biederman (Addison Wesley, 1997). Bennis declares the age of the empowered individual ended: what matters now is "collaborative advantage" and the assembling of powerful teams. Drawing from six case studies that include Xerox's PARC labs, the 1992 Clinton campaign, and Disney animation studios, Bennis and coauthor Patricia Biederman distill the characteristics of successful collaboration, showing how talent can be pooled and managed for greater results than any individual is capable of producing.

The Fifth Discipline: The Art & Practice of the Learning Organization, Peter M. Senge (Doubleday Currency, 1990). The best book on organizational learning we know of at the time of writing.

Measure Up! How to Measure Corporate Performance, **2nd ed.**, Richard L. Lynch and Kelvin F. Cross (Blackwell, 1995). A complete guide to designing and implementing a strategically driven, closed-loop, balanced scorecard.

Corporate Renaissance: The Art of Reengineering, Richard L. Lynch et al. (Blackwell, 1994). A practical guide to process design.

Intelligent Enterprise, James Brian Quinn (Free Press, 1992). Quinn argues that the successful companies of the 1990s – whether in manufacturing or services – will derive their real competitive advantage not from ephemerally superior products but from deep knowledge of highly developed skills such as design, research, marketing, and management of capital.

Competing by Design: The Power of Organizational Architecture, David A. Nadler and Michael L. Tushman (Oxford University Press, 1997). A case of design of organizational and communications structures around Mission and Process.

Designing Organizations, Jay R. Galbraith (Jossey-Bass, 1995). Drawing on over ten years of research, the author shows how organization design supports policies, behaviors, and performance. The book will equip leaders with the concrete understanding and tools necessary to select and implement the most efficient design and to create a superior organization.

Adaptive Enterprise, Stephan Haeckel (Harvard Business School Press, 1999). Haeckel outlines the new sense-and-respond business model that helps companies anticipate, adapt, and respond to continually changing customer needs and industry forces. In fact, he argues, the only kind of strategy that makes sense in the face of change is a strategy to become adaptive.

Built to Last, James C. Collins and Jerry I. Porras (HarperBusiness, 1994). Based on a groundbreaking and influential research project, which has begun to fundamentally change the way in which executives think about long-term success. Companies share a number of distinct characteristics: Core values that never change, a purpose beyond profits, and a relentless drive to change and improve everything except their core values.

Integrated Management Systems, Thomas H. Lee, Shoji Shiba, and Robert Chapman Wood (Wiley, 1999). Based on a profoundly important six-year study by the Center for the Quality of Management (CQM), *Integrated Management Systems* shows how successful organizations accomplish something unbelievably powerful: creating their own particular ways of executing the scientific method.

The Boundaryless Organization: Breaking the Chains of Organizational Structure, Ron Ashkenas, Dave Ulrich, Todd Jick, and Steve Kerr (Jossey-Bass, 1995). Calling all businesses, the proactive business management guide to bursting boundaries in all directions – vertical, horizontal, external, and geographic.

Lean Thinking: Banish Waste and Create Wealth in Your Corporation, James P. Womack and Daniel T. Jones (Simon & Schuster, 1996). This is a ground-level presentation on what waste is, how to spot it, and what to do about it. The key message is Shared Attitude and Clear Thinking about improvement, and especially about focused improvement targets.

Working Knowledge, Thomas H. Davenport and Laurence Prusak (Harvard Business School Press, 1998. Strong insights into development and benefiting from knowledge capital.

The Quality Secret, William E. Conway (Conway Quality, 1992). An early work on waste elimination. Gets to the nuts and bolts of the process and provides a people, process, and technology viewpoint.

ABC of Architecture, James F. O'Gorman (Penn, 1998). The essence of architecture and how it relates time, space, form, and function.

"A Framework for Information Systems Architecture," John A. Zachman (*IBM Systems Journal*, 28, 3, 1987). The seminal and still timely work on IS Architecture.

"Extending and Formalizing the Framework for Information Systems Architecture," John A. Zachman and John F. Sowa (*IBM Systems Journal*, 31, 3, 1992). Adds new dimensions and more structure to the method.

Bibliography

Ackoff, Russell L., *Creating the Corporate Future: Plan or be Planned For* (John Wiley, 1981).

Albrecht, Karl, *Northbound Train* (American Management Association, 1994).

Ashkenas, Ron, Dave Ulrich, Todd Jick, and Steve Kerr, *The Boundaryless Organization: Breaking the Chains of Organizational Structure* (Jossey-Bass, 1995).

Beckhard, Richard, and Wendy Pritchard, *Changing the Essence: The Art of Creating and Leading Fundamental Change in Organizations* (Jossey-Bass, 1992).

Bennis, Warren, *On Becoming a Leader* (Addison Wesley, 1994).

Bennis, Warren, and Patricia Biederman, *Organizing Genius: The Secrets of Creative Collaboration* (Addison Wesley, 1997).

Collins, James C., and Jerry I. Porras, *Built to Last* (HarperBusiness, 1994).

Conway, William E., *The Quality Secret* (Conway Quality, 1992).

Davenport, Thomas, *Process Innovation: Reengineering Work Through Information Technology* (Harvard Business School Press, 1992).

Davenport, Thomas H., and Laurence Prusak, *Working Knowledge* (Harvard Business School Press, 1998).

Drucker, Peter F., *Innovation & Entrepreneurship: Practice & Principles* (HarperCollins, 1986).

Galbraith, Jay R., *Designing Organizations* (Jossey-Bass, 1995).

Greene, Robert, and Joost Elffers, *The 48 Laws of Power* (Viking, 1998).

Haeckel, Stephan, *Adaptive Enterprise* (Harvard Business School Press, 1999).

Juran, Joseph M., *Managerial Breakthrough: A New Concept of the Manager's Job* (McGraw Hill, 1964).

Kotter, John P., *Leading Change* (Harvard Business School Press, 1996).

Lee, Thomas H., Shoji Shiba, and Robert Chapman Wood, *Integrated Management Systems* (Wiley, 1999).

Lynch, Richard L., and Kelvin F. Cross, *Measure Up! How to Measure Corporate Performance*, 2nd ed. (Blackwell, 1995).

Lynch, Richard L., et al., *Corporate Renaissance: The Art of Reengineering* (Blackwell, 1994).

Nadler, David A., and Michael L. Tushman, *Competing by Design: The Power of Organizational Architecture* (Oxford University Press, 1997).

Norris, Grant, et al., *E-Business and ERP: Transforming the Enterprise* (Wiley, 2000).

O'Gorman, James F., *ABC of Architecture* (Penn, 1998).

Quinn, James Brian, *Intelligent Enterprise* (Free Press, 1992).

Senge, Peter M., *The Fifth Discipline: The Art & Practice of the Learning Organization* (Doubleday Currency, 1990).

Shiba, Shoji, Alan Graham, and David Walden, *A New American TQM* (Productivity Press, 1993).

Smallwood, W. Norman, Lee Tom Perry, and Randall G. Scott, *Real-Time Strategy* (Wiley, 1993).

Ulrich, David, and Norm Smallwood, *Why the Bottom Line Isn't* (Wiley, 2003).

Ulrich, David, Jack Zenger, and Norm Smallwood, *Results-Based Leadership* (Harvard Business School Press, 1999).

Wheatly, Margaret J., *Leadership and the New Science* (Berret-Koehler, 1992).

Womack, James P., and Daniel T. Jones, *Lean Thinking: Banish Waste and Create Wealth in Your Corporation* (Simon & Schuster, 1996).

Zachman, John A., "A Framework for Information Systems Architecture," *IBM Systems Journal*, 28, 3 (1987).

Zachman, John A., and John F. Sowa, "Extending and Formalizing the Framework for Information Systems Architecture," *IBM Systems Journal*, 31, 3 (1992).

Glossary

Advantage work

Work that creates distinction and competitive advantage.

Archetypes

A model, type, or style after which other things are patterned. For example, in residential buildings, "colonial" and "contemporary" are two different archetypes. Each suggests different doors, windows, and furnishings. In business management, style, organization structure, and process design are archetypes that, depending on the model chosen, suggest different tactical choices. The use of archetypes accelerates execution and assures interoperability of the individual components.

Architectural requirements

A framework increasing the level of assurance that conflicts among elements of the organization are not being created. They establish guidelines that potential solutions shall not violate (without explicit management approval) and offer steerage toward the selection of optimized solutions.

Architecture, building

The way that the components of a building come together and produce a serviceable space.

Architecture, business

The way that the components of a business come together and produce and execute its strategy. When various archetypes are shaped to respond to a particular set of drivers and support a particular set of capabilities, we refer to the resulting set of guidelines as business architecture.

Attributes

Knowledge, skills, and/or traits that enable leaders to produce desired business results.

Balanced scorecard

A balanced scorecard does not mean the same number of weights in predefined categories such as customer or investor. It refers more to the balance in the business agenda. Scorecard models share a similar logic:

- to achieve financial success companies must satisfy customers;
- to satisfy customers, organizations must optimize internal value-creating processes;
- to optimize processes, organizations must learn and their employees must grow individual competencies.

Best practice

The establishment of a process or procedure that produces superior, repeatable results.

Business capabilities

What the company needs to be able to do to execute its business strategy (e.g., support customers through any medium – telephone, fax, the Web, etc.). These capabilities are operational in nature.

Business focus

The company's predominant business strength: e.g., product, customer/markets, technology, production capacity, or distribution.

Business life cycle

Represents the evolution a business goes through as products and service mature.

Business life cycle; improve

Continuous process improvement, e.g., Six Sigma or TQM processes.

Business life cycle; maintain

Stay on track to process standards. Focus on cost reduction, efficient support work, and parity in consumer-specific capabilities; i.e., speed or quality.

Business life cycle; regenerate

Create new business opportunities, business model innovation, technology innovation, and new process design.

Business life cycle; survive

Run the business. Focus on cost control and cash management.

Business necessity work

Those activities that need to be performed an industry parity and at low cost.

Business strategy

Determines the way that a specific business will create distinctiveness, including the products it offers, the markets it serves, and the capabilities required to execute the strategy.

Capabilities

See **Business capabilities; Organization capabilities.**

Change driver

An individual, compelling group of change forces that will act as a lever upon the company and force it to alter the way it does business.

Change forces

Those external and internal forces that are impacting the enterprise and may require it to move.

Continual business alignment

A low-cost, highly iterative process that takes vision to action:

- aligns business, process, technology, and organizational strategies to improve operational capability;
- defines the essential capabilities required to sustain long-term enterprise profitability and target the critical short-term initiatives that realize those capabilities;
- outlines the rapid deployment of a three-month program-integration cycle.

Core process

All the functions and the sequence of activities (regardless of where they reside in the organization), policies and procedures, and supporting systems required to meet a marketplace need through a specific strategy. It includes all functions involved in the development, production, and provision of specific products or services to particular customers. In other words, emphasis is given to workflow, not to organization charts. New product introduction, order fulfillment, and customer service are examples of what we mean by "core process."

Core values

A set of deeply held beliefs that unify and inspire employees. They define how employees see themselves and their employers.

Corporate strategy

Defines the relationships among businesses in the corporation portfolio. It defines the domain of businesses in a portfolio, the boundaries of those businesses, and the process by which investments will be determined among the alternative businesses.

Customer life cycle

The process of acquiring customers and keeping them.

Customer life cycle; attract

Finding potential customers – channel development, brand management, product marketing, advertising, promotion, data mining.

Customer life cycle; convert

Closing prospects to sales needs assessment, value proposition, and solution proposal.

Customer life cycle; fulfill

Completing orders – process technology, customization, distribution, and e-commerce.

Customer life cycle; leverage

Cross selling, product enhancements, training, customer research.

Customer measures

Key value proposition measures: quality, delivery, and price

Customer relationship management

A comprehensive set of processes and technologies that deal with how customers are treated in the customer-facing business processes, especially those involved in attracting customers, converting prospects/browsers to customers, and fulfilling needs and customer service.

Customer value proposition

The predominant way to be recognized by customers: quality, innovation, service, speed, or price.

Employee measures

The measures around capability and commitment: e.g., turnover measures, productivity, etc.

Flexibility option

Investments generate interaction and provide options not previously possible.

Functional competencies

The technical skills needed to perform a job (e.g., grasp of fiber-optic technology or a software language).

Growth option

Investment creates future growth options above and beyond the returns generated by the initial investment.

Intangible value

The premium paid in stock price, based on factors such as quality of management, technology, etc.

Investor measures

Key financial and market-share data: e.g., profits, sales, relative market share.

Lag indicator

The dependent variables on the scorecard, such as market share and financial numbers. Their score is determined by the lead indicators.

Lead indicator

Balanced scorecard projects are predicated on the assumption that employee measures on commitment and capability will lead to desired organizational capabilities, such as new product time-to-market, which in turn lead to customer results in terms of quality, delivery, and price. These measures are the independent variables at the business-process level that drive the investor or financial/market results at the business unit or corporate level (i.e., the dependent variables). In other words, companies need to focus on the non-financial indicators at all levels, because they represent the collective wisdom of the organization on what measures will improve the odds of success.

Leadership

The art of visioning, setting direction, providing inspiration, and mobilizing an organization. A longer-term view. *Compare* **Management**.

Leadership brand

The premium price in the market that leadership commands.

Leadership, effective

Leadership Attributes X Results.

Management

The act of controlling and maintaining systems and structures. Focus is more short-term and tactical. *Compare* **Leadership**.

Measurement system

The collection of measures that provide feedback on the performance of the system and its parts. It is important to view measures as part of a system – just like the human body – how is everything performs together is what counts.

Measures

The results, dimension, quantity, or capacity of a business. Understanding performance characteristics requires an understanding of the business processes that deliver value.

Mission

In general terms, this describes what business(es) the company is in. It describes what the company will do, what benefits it will deliver, to whom, and to what extent.

Non-value-added work

Inspections, test, moves, rework, etc.

Organization capabilities

How the organization achieves its business capabilities. These capabilities need to exist throughout every aspect of the business.

Organization measures

Key measures around learning, speed accountability, boundarylessness; e.g., time to market, percentage of milestones achieved.

Performance measurement systems

A *measurement system* is the collection of measures that provide feedback on the performance of the system and its parts. It is important to view measures as part of a system – just like the human body – how everything is performing together is what counts.

Processes

Processes are the way that the enterprise conducts business.

Projects

The way that processes are created, improved, and removed.

Purpose

Why the company exists and what it stands for (beyond profits).

Real options; business

See **Growth option, Staging option, Flexibility option**.

Service level agreements (SLAs)

Contracts between service providers and customers that define the services provided, the metrics associated with the services, acceptable and unacceptable service levels, liabilities on the part of the service provider and customer, and actions to be taken in specific circumstances.

Staging option

Investment in stages rather than all at once, allowing decisions (new options) at critical junctures.

Strategic support work

Work that enables competitive advantage.

Strategy

See **Corporate strategy, Business strategy**.

Types of work

Work can be classified as either *advantage* (the work that creates distinction), *strategic support* (the work that enables competitive advantage), or *business necessity* (those activities that need to be performed at industry parity and at low cost). Collectively these are called types of work (TOW). TOW is not the same as the traditional *value-added analysis*, but is a filter above it. For example, there is *value-added work* and non-value work in advantage, strategic support, and business-necessity processes.

Value-added analysis

The study of work that determines if the product or service has been done right the first time. Non-value-adding activity related to rework and inspection can be quantified in terms of lost time and money. *Compare* **Types of work**.

Value exchange system

How a company exchanges value among shareholders and customers.

Vision

This paints a compelling and inspirational picture of where the company will be (an ideal state) at some future date (when), intimating how the company will look, feel and be.

Work activities

The day-to-day activities that drive processes to deliver business value and drive projects to change the way in which the company conducts business.

Work-out

A deeply engrained and internalized process for addressing and solving its problems – quickly, simply, and with the involvement of people who will ultimately carry out the decision (Ulrich).

Index

technology architecture, 123, 174
TeleTech., 8, 22, 102
transformation type, 172
Travelocity, 105
Tuchman, Ken, 3, 106
Tushman, Michael, 117–18
Tyco, 16, 61, 136
types of work, 66–70

vertical boundary, 23–4
Viacom, 8, 30
Virgin Airlines, 65
vision, 39–41

Wang, Dr. An, 22
Wang Laboratories, 22, 29
Welch, Jack, 4–5, 16, 23, 26–7
Whitmore, Kay, 17
Work-Out, 4, 23, 190
Worldcom, 16

Xerox, 58, 108

Zachman, John, 122–4
Zeien, Al, 16